Phantoms & Monsters

Cryptid Encounters

Lon Strickler

Triangulum Publishing

Copyright © 2016 by Lon Strickler

ISBN 13: 978-1530304578

ISBN10: 1530304571

First published (ebook) September 25, 2012.

Edited by Ash Staunton

7

Dedicated.

To Vanessa, who owns my heart.
To Adrienne, Matthew and Kayli, who are my soul.
To my friends, colleagues and readers for their support.

The cases in this book are a collection of personal accounts and anecdotes submitted to me by regular people who felt compelled to search for answers about their strange encounters.

Contact the author at:

www.phantomsandmonsters.com

lonstrickler@phantomsandmonsters.com

I've been interested in the strange and unusual for as long as I can remember. My childhood included many bicycle jaunts to the Gettysburg battlefield and other odd locations that would draw my attention. After a while, I started to realize that I was sensitive to spiritual energies that would occasionally surface, sometimes manifesting into apparitions that would continue performing soldiers' duties. Muffled sounds of drums, gunfire, cannons and mortal suffering were not uncommon. As well, the smell of gunpowder, blood and death hung in the air like morning fog. I never got used to the horrible sensations though I was fascinated by the opportunity to witness the phenomena before me.

Not long after I graduated from high school, I became interested in investigating paranormal events. In the 1970's, a person who studied the paranormal was looked upon as demented and mentally unbalanced, but I continued to explore locations that were supposedly haunted. During this period, I was aware of cryptozoology but I had little interest in searching for undocumented creatures. My perspective suddenly changed one morning in May 1981, when I had an encounter that changed my life forever. It wouldn't be the last time I experienced a being that could not explain.

The following collection of personal accounts and anecdotes were submitted to me by regular people who felt compelled to search for answers about their strange encounters. I have learned to keep an open mind when reading and discussing witness accounts because I truly understand how they feel. Few people believed me either.

Lon Strickler

Chapter 1

My interest in cryptozoology began the day I witnessed a creature that was beyond my belief or, what I thought, the boundaries of reality. The incident was reported to a BFRO investigator several years ago in hope that they may be able to get further information from local authorities. Unfortunately, this investigator was unable to help.

The date of the encounter was May 9, 1981 about 10:00 am and I was fly-fishing for redeye and smallmouth bass on the south branch of the Patapsco River approximately 1 mile downstream from Rt.32 near Sykesville, Maryland. The weather was sunny and slightly breezy and the air temperature was in the low 60's. This section of river flattens out into riffles then empties into a larger pool, an area I had fished several times previously.

I was on the south bank near the riffles when I noticed a stray mixed breed dog sniffing around the weeds and thickets on the north bank. The dog was about 50 yards from me and was weaving in and out of the brush. I wasn't worried about the dog bothering me, so I just put it out of my mind and concentrated on fishing.

After a few minutes or so, I heard the dog barking and growling. I figured that he stirred up a deer, but when I looked at the direction of the ruckus I noticed a dark hairy creature bobbing up and down in the thickets. I stopped fishing and moved closer to the riffles to get a better look and noticed that the dog stopped barking. Suddenly, I heard a loud yelp from the dog and the creature stood up. The best I could tell is that this "thing" was about 7-8 ft. tall and had dark matted hair. I could only see the body from the chest up because the rest of the body was obscured by the weeds and thickets. I stood completely still and could hear a series of "tick" sounds while observing this creature walk slowly through the thickets towards the woods. I started to follow it and in the meantime I noticed a strong musky scent that reminded me of fox urine.

I had waders on so I could only move so fast in an attempt to get a better look at this creature. It simply moved too fast for me. I decided to go back to my car, drive into Sykesville and make an immediate report to the authorities. On my way back to the vehicle, I noticed the dog and it had noticeable blood around the neck and hind area but seemed to be able to get around. I figured I better stay away for the dog regardless.

I drove to the nearest telephone which was located outside a bar. The local police told me to go back to the area and they would meet me there. So I got back into the car (I seriously thought about going into the bar for a minute first, but better judgment made me change my mind) and started to drive back to the river. I was amazed that a Maryland State Police cruiser was already there. The State Police officer told to get back in my car and leave immediately because they didn't know how dangerous the situation was. I tried to explain to him that I made the initial report, but he refused to let me talk and again told me to leave. I went back to the area about 1 hour later and the place was crawling with people and many state and other official vehicles. One man standing near the road did tell me that someone found some hair samples but refused to say anything else.

For many years, I tried to gather information from local authorities in regards to this incident, but I have always been told that "no information is available" or "we have no report of an incident". Since that time, I have decided that I would do my own investigations and find information on my own.

I later received this comment to this incident (unedited):

"This sure brings up some old memories. I always expected that sooner or later it would get out. I'm glad someone else saw it and kicked over the can. I'll add beans.

I was one of the responders on that call. Right after we'd closed down the road a government response team arrived. Those guys weren't fooling around. Their big dogs and bigger guns made that evident. It wasn't long before we were locked out: ordered into our cruisers and away from the area. The "into our cruisers" part was the weirdest. We were outmanned, outgunned and outranked by the feds who had taken over. Soon after that, within an hour at most, several choppers were overhead, as in three. It was a manhunt on a larger scale than we could have mustered so quickly, and that is saying a lot.

I've never really been positive what happened. None of our guys had actually seen "it," though I imagine "it" was caught or killed. They said there were hair samples and footprint photos and casts taken. We were debriefed and basically instructed not to speak of this matter. With that

I'll close and say no more except that it did happen as described on here."

At the time, I called the being I witnessed a 'Bigfoot' because, frankly, that was the only way I could have described it. It wasn't human, it wasn't an ape. For over 30 years my encounter with this being had left a strange hole in my understanding of nature and reality.

Over the years, I have tried to gather more information on my sighting as well as other sightings in the general area. Since my sighting in 1981 there have been two (2) more BFRO 'Class A' reports along the Patapsco River Valley and another four (4) general reports and sightings in the same area from 1972-1979.

The 'Sykesville Monster'

I interviewed and got to know several of the witnesses of the 1972-73 'Sykesville Monster' flap after my personal encounter in 1981. Many of these witnesses have since passed away. There were other unreported incidents in the general Sykesville and Gaither, MD areas. I personally took statements to eight (8) more sightings / encounters between 1972-1979, including a home invasion on Norris Ave. and a utility shed break-in on Oklahoma Ave. Both were located in Sykesville. There were also several chicken pens broke into up and down the South Branch of the Patapsco River in Gaither MD, Sykesville MD, Woodstock MD, Daniels MD and Ellicott City, MD. Most of the sightings have been within the Patapsco State Park, which has a history of unusual activity (UFO, paranormal and cryptid) throughout the park. I still live within 15 miles of all the locations.

I decided to come to grips with my encounter and had a sketch or image of the being's face created. I knew that if the image was similar to what I actually witnessed there would be controversy and doubters, but I couldn't let that bother me.

After making a few inquiries, I was directed to a retired police forensics artist who was a private investigator in Florida. I forwarded all the facial descriptions that I had gathered from the witness' sightings and subsequent interviews. I received the image with a note from the artist that read "are you sure this is what you witnessed? It looks like a rendering of early man except for a few features." I called him and assured him that this is what I witnessed, this is what we all witnessed. This was the 'Sykesville Monster.'

A few years after my Bigfoot encounter I happened upon an older gentleman named Phil who was fishing on Piney Run near Marriottsville, MD. I had been trying out a new fly rod upstream and confronted Phil as he was packing up gear by his car. We started talking about a few odds and ends when he mentioned that skeletal remains of a large 'human' had been found on the Piney Run south bank not far from where we were standing. He said that another fisherman had chanced upon the bones while he wandered off the trail. After the discovery the man simply mentioned to a few other fishermen that there were bones in that direction as he gestured to the area.

Phil said that he and a companion walked over to the other side of the stream to take a look at the remains. He said that some of the bones were obviously missing but there was a skull without a jawbone as well as the vertebrae, a few ribs and long bones of the arms and legs. There was no visible tissue but there were a few small desiccated patches of reddish brown fur scattered around. Phil said that both he and his companion both muttered at the same time, "Where are the clothes?" Then Phil said, "This is too big to be a human."

This was back in the early 1980's so there were no cell phones. Phil's companion walked to the small store by the Patapsco River Bridge to call the police. As they waited for the authorities Phil took out his fish tape and measured the upper arm bone (Humerus) he remembered it measure 22 inches. Phil's observations and conclusions were that it was something similar to a large ape or gorilla. He also mentioned that the skull looked very much human but larger.

After the Baltimore County Police and State Police arrived on the scene everyone was advised to leave the area. In fact, Phil said they placed crime scene tape across the road so no one could get within 300 yards of the location. He said he and a few others hung around the general store by the railroad tracks so they could see who was coming and going from the scene. There were unmarked helicopters bringing people on-site as well as several unmarked vehicles. These vehicles were similar to what I had seen after my encounter. There was never any mention on the local news.

As a result of the information I gathered from witnesses and residents I assume that there may have been a breeding population of Bigfoot in the Patapsco State Park. The most recent sighting was in 1993 by an 8 year old boy in the Woodstock, MD area, a few miles downriver from Marriottsville. There was a report filed for a sighting in 2001 at the Liberty Reservoir (witnesses thought they saw Bigfoot on frozen lake). Since the area is now heavily zoned for residential dwellings, it's obvious to me that these creature breeding units have moved on to more natural locations.

Chapter 2

When I started publishing the 'Phantoms & Monsters' blog in 2006, I had hoped it would become an enjoyable 'read' for paranormal enthusiasts. As time went on, I soon realized that there were many more people experiencing unexplained phenomena than I had previously thought.

Many of the stories and anecdotes in this collection have previously been published on the blog.

[Please note: For the most part, the accounts will remain in the first-person and unedited as reported to me.]

Hominid Sighting Reported Near Red Lion, York County, Pennsylvania - July 18, 2008.

I received a telephone call today from a woman who claims to have seen a small bigfoot-like creature on July 18th, 2008 near the town of Red Lion, Pa. She stated that she had been shopping and was on her way home. As she was driving south on Rt. 624 about 2 miles from Red Lion, she noticed something running across a field near a home construction site. At first, she thought it was a large dog but it stood upright like a human. She pulled her car into an unfinished side road and observed the creature for several minutes as it would stop, look around, then it would continue running until it reached a small woods. She states that it was around 7 p.m. in the evening and clear.

She described it as stocky with muscular arms and legs and no more than 4 foot in stature and sparsely covered in dark gray hair. It had no clothes though she could not determine the gender. At one point, she says that she was near enough to notice the head was smaller than that of a human child of the same height. She said that only one other person (a neighbor) was told of this sighting and that she did not want any notoriety. Her only reason for contacting me was because she had seen my blog and that I lived nearby (about 50 miles south in Baltimore) and thought I may want to check the area out for myself.

She only gave me the name 'Macy' as a reference (I assume this is not her actual name) and refused to disclose her address and other personal information. There have been Bigfoot sighting reports in this area of Pennsylvania in the past as well as in neighboring Maryland. This very well could have been a juvenile Bigfoot. There have been local and Indian legends of a small hominid (the Albatwitch) in Lancaster and York Counties. The 'Albatwitch' is a small (about four feet tall), manlike creature which supposedly lived in wooded areas. Their main area of residence seemed to be near Chickies Rock, a heavily wooded area along the banks of the Susquehanna River about a mile or two north of Columbia, Pa. Albatwitches were also reported from wooded areas all along the river's shore and were said to be fond of apples thus their bizarre common name is short for "apple-snitch."

Legend also says that the albatwitches either became extinct or were driven nearly into extinction in the later years of the nineteenth century. Chickies Rock, where the creatures supposedly lived, does have a tradition of strange sights and sounds. In the 1950s and 1970s, a man-like figure was seen several times, and local legends also speak of sounds like the crack of a whip heard in the woods at night.

Several sightings of Bigfoot-type beings have been recorded from this area. A vague report concerning the sighting of a hairy humanoid came from Lancaster in 1973. Lancaster is 10 miles east of Columbia. Another came from the town of North Annville (about 20 miles to the north) in the same year. In addition, a number of reports have surfaced out of neighboring York County, where Red Lion is located.

'Wild Man' Near Strasburg, Lancaster County, Pennsylvania - August 1978 – afternoon.

Three Amish men were working in their field when an odd looking man approached them from the direction of a neighboring farm. The man was yelling and jumping about. The Amish men were alarmed and noticed that this 'man' had arms, legs and a face that seemed different, more animal than human. He had coarse dark hair on his limbs and face and wore what appeared to be a dark colored and tattered pair of old style boxer shorts. As the man-creature approached closer, he was yelling something but it was not understood by the men.

The men ran towards their house, the man-creature was right behind them. One of the Amish men ducked into the dairy barn and the other two immediately went in the house. An elderly Amish woman, who had been in the garden, came to see what was going on. When the man-creature saw her it suddenly stopped running, sat down on the grass and remained quiet while staring at the sky.

The men came out of the house and one of them slowly walked over to the man-creature and attempted to talk to it. The man-creature continued to look at the sky but started to mumble. The man and woman noticed that a horrible stench permeated from this creature, described at rotting flesh.

After several minutes, the creature got to its feet and started to walk towards the dairy barn. As it did, the witnesses noticed that the creature started to 'fade away.' Eventually it completely disappeared from view just before it reached the barn. Shocked, the Amish witnesses dropped to their knees, not knowing what they had witnessed.

[Note: this account was communicated by one of the witnesses to a non-Amish friend who periodically purchased produce from them. It was disclosed to me several years after the incident though I do know of the location and who two of the witnesses were (I was raised in the general area). The other witnesses have since passed away. The witness who gave the account still lives at the location and has (reluctantly) verified the incident to me. In turn, I promised to keep personal information confidential.]

Historically, Wild Men and/or Bigfoot-like creatures have become part of the Lancaster / York County folklore. There have been sightings as old as the earliest settlers in this area as well as the Susquehannock people who inhabited the land previously.

In 1987, I had a conversation with a self-described shaman whose Susquehannock relatives had moved to Ohio after many others were killed off by smallpox and invading settlers. The Susquehannocks were said to be 'giants' by John Smith and the early settlers. Most were described as being 'well over six foot high' and broad-chested. This shaman told me that the Susquehannocks had placed a curse on the land before they left and that the dead would rise as shape shifters and torment the white man.

Oh-Mah, the 'Boss of the Woods.'

I received the following email on November 5th, 2008:
"My question to you is; have I seen something unusual?"

In August of 2006, I was working in Northern California and was interested in finding Bigfoot prints. I have a friend who is a member of the Hoopa First Nation. I contacted him and then spoke to an elder. I was taken to an area where some footprints had just been found. Being skeptical, I took my right boot off and stepped down next to the foot print. I am 7' 1" tall and weigh 395 pounds and wear a size 17 street shoe or a size 19 boot (as boot sizes are often mislabeled). I am of Scot and Lakota Sioux lineage and speak a number of First Nation languages.

After putting on my boots, we heard a screaming howl. My friends started saying Oh-mah was coming and we had to leave. My friend Dave told his elder about what I had done and we went back to the site three hours later. There were numerous large footprints surrounding mine and what I believe to be a large finger hole in the middle of my footprint.

I was contacted a couple of weeks later and invited back to the reservation as they normally lose a good portion of their apple crop to Oh-mah but in 2006 they didn't lose anything. They wanted to know if I could come back every year and walk around barefoot to intimidate Oh-mah and if I have any big friends my size.

Oh-mah either saw me with the much shorter native indians and thought I was another Oh-mah or recognized the footprint as a threat. The elder thought Oh-mah didn't want a confrontation with something almost as big as he and left the area.

The Oh-mah footprint was the same length as mine but an inch and half wider at the ball and 3/4 of an inch wider at the heel. The depth of the print was the same.

I have spoken with some so-called experts from the BFRO and from the Bigfoot Discovery Project and got laughed at but then they wanted me to come with them and speak to the Bigfoot via bull horn in either native language. I rather not be used by someone who is too narrow minded for me to speak to the kononpaiochis (literally the people of the north who don't comb their hair - Bigfoot)." Sincerely yours, DTWOC.

[Note: I have been told that the native tribes in this area (Hupa and Yurok) both use the name 'Omah' or 'Oh-mah' translated as 'boss of the woods.']

The 'Stick Breakers.'

"During the spring of 2003, I was visiting my sister who lives in Hampstead, New Hampshire. She lives in a somewhat wooded subdivision. It was early spring in New England and the weather had been a fairly rainy. I would frequently go outside by myself to smoke cigarettes late at night, on the porch after midnight. While I was outside I would hear larger sticks crack and break on the forest floor near where I was sitting but no leaves rustling. At first I didn't think much of it. I am a seasoned camper and just didn't think it was a big deal, I figured it was just an animal of some kind. This happened night after night. Then I noticed the sounds of something dropping out of the trees and an animal or being of some kind scraping on the bark a bit as it descended. I tried looking for movement but saw nothing, like an animal or anything. The flood lights were on every time I was out there and were brightly shining; there was a street light at the end of the long paved driveway off in the distance. On subsequent nights I took a flashlight and tried to shine whatever animal it might be with but that was to no avail. Even though everything was brightly lit I saw nothing at all.

I tried this night after night. The sounds were there every single evening without fail. I could hear them moving closer and closer to me the longer I was out there. During the day I looked for tracks and marks on trees or other evidence but didn't turn up a thing. I picked up sticks and broke a few to see what size stick I was hearing. I ascertained that the stick diameter was about an inch. I had my 11 yr. old nephew go out in the woods to jump on sticks and see if he could break some of them, so I could check the way it sounds from where I was sitting, trying to judge the distance. He jumped on some but because they were kind of moist he could only break the smaller ones. He weighed only about 75 to 80 pounds. This told me that whatever it is, weighs more than that.

I could break the bigger ones by jumping on them, but I weigh 150 pounds. There are no animals in that area that are really large and could break that size stick based on the tests I did. Whatever it was would move in close to me, so I used the nephew to run around and make similar noises to gauge the distance in the daylight when they were at their closest. They were about 20-30 feet from me at best. I know there was more than one of them because I could hear one back beside the house and another one was in the front at the end of the driveway. They moved in very close to where I was and I could hear them coming from two different directions. They were not visible with the naked eye at all. I tried to take some digital photos but saw nothing discernible in the pictures.

Another thing that happened, my sister didn't have any window coverings downstairs, she loved the view of the trees, and I would sit at night on her computer surfing the web and chatting online near those windows. I frequently would get the feeling that someone was watching me. I wrote it off as just my imagination. Then there was the issue of the dogs barking and howling every night real late like they were hearing something. They were kept in crates in the basement at night. They would start their howling and wouldn't stop unless someone would go down there and make them stop. They also would look out the windows late in the evening and start barking out behind the house as tough something was there. We all thought it was just another animal or whatever, and wrote it off. My brother in law decided to keep the dogs upstairs with him at night to keep them quiet.

I was outside one night very late after midnight alone. I was up on her porch near the door. I heard them coming again. The flood lights were on and I could see well into the trees because there weren't too many smaller bushes in the way. I saw nothing but still heard them. No rustling only sticks breaking. My sis had a few planters with flowers in them on a lower landing from where I was standing. It was in the really bright light from the flood lights and was only about 8 to 10 feet from me.

Some of the flowers in the planter draped over the side and hung out away from the planters. As I stood there I watched the plants move to one side and then flop back as though something had brushed past them, only nothing was there that I could see at all. There were no other sounds, like footsteps or grinding pebbles or grit. No wind at all. When the flowers swung, and they moved a lot not just a little. Whatever it was would have to come up the stairs to get me. I stood there shocked, sort of and running over what I had just seen in my mind briefly, and got freaked out completely, went inside quickly and locked the door. Everyone else was asleep in the house. I looked out the side window and saw nothing.

Another late evening I was on the computer and I got that feeling of being watched again I looked into the living room from where I was sitting and I thought I saw shadows on the ceiling as though someone had walked past the lamps in there. I thought I must be just really tired and told myself it was my imagination. I decided to take a hot shower to relax before bed. The bathroom door is right across from the basement door.

The basement door was closed when I went in to shower and everyone was in bed asleep upstairs with the lights off. When I came out of the shower the basement door was open and I just closed it thinking it was a bit strange but no big deal. Then I went to go upstairs and I saw my 11 year old nephew's bedroom light was on and I got scared. I went up the stairs and he was in bed dead asleep but the light was on real bright. I became afraid for the kids and went and woke my brother-in-law up. He blew me off and went back to sleep. Just then my niece woke up to let her dog out to go potty so I asked her to sit up with me for a while. Thank God she was there to sit and keep me company for a little while.

What I am saying here is I believe these things were coming in the house somehow and that's why the dogs barked and howled like they did. I am not sure how they got in, maybe through the walls, maybe the basement outside door, I don't know, but I feel they were coming in. What are these things? Aliens? Dimensional entities? Were they just watching us? Were they abducting? Testing? Or even hunting? I have no idea and it's frightening! If you think about it you realize that on the grass there are no sticks to break, so they are quiet or silent, and there they were right up next to the house! How many other houses did they go into too?!

Then the story goes a bit further, my sister later divorced and started dating again. Her new boyfriend and I were talking on the phone one evening recently, and the subject turned to the paranormal. I knew he is an avid New Hampshire hunter. So, I asked him if he had ever heard of anything like this. He said yes!!! He said that once, in November of 2003, he and five of his friends were out hunting on White Mountain one year and all of them were of course armed. They had set up camp for the night and made a fire. As they all were sitting around (after midnight) getting settled for the evening they started hearing "the stick breakers," breaking sticks all around them but not rustling leaves at all.

They didn't see anything at all, and couldn't figure out what it was. They did try to shine their flashlights and see what it was but they couldn't see anything at all. All five got spooked and decided to turn in for the night and when morning came they decided to move their camp farther up the mountain closer to where they knew a larger group was set up. They all decided to not talk about the event after that day and they decided to never go back again either!!! I was so glad to hear that someone else had experienced the "stick breakers"! Now at least I know I am not nuts. I know there are others out there who have had similar experiences, so, please step up and let's hear your story!

I feel that this needs to be brought to the public's attention and put on record.

I will be trying to establish whether these things are still out there or not. In case that they are, I would like someone to go there and use thermal photography, or IR to see if these things can be seen somehow, filmed or photographed or recorded. I have no funds to buy the equipment necessary to do it myself, though I'd love to! I need to find someone who might be willing to go there and shoot some film in that area. Bring their equipment and check it out." Thanks, S.O.

Yeti Encounter.

"During the Christmas break in grad school in December 1983-January 1984, I was part of an Everest trek. We weren't going to summit, basically we hiked from a small mountain town airstrip to the base camp at the Khumbu Glacier where the real climbers take off from. It takes 10 days or so each way, with stops at monasteries along the way to adjust to the altitude.

It was winter in Nepal so most of the higher elevations were basically deserted. It's very cold and rocky up there, not very inviting, but starkly beautiful. The pack train had gone on ahead to set up camp and we each just hiked along at our own pace until we caught up at the end of the day. It was mid-afternoon and as I rounded a sharp corner in the tiny, narrow mountain ledge trail I encountered a creature standing on the trail in front of an ice fall.

It was clearly a primate of some sort. Not huge, between three and four feet tall. Thick reddish hair, like an orangutan, and with long arms. We just sort of looked one another over for maybe 10 seconds and then he turned, climbed up the ice fall (maybe 20-25 feet) and vanished over the top. I didn't feel threatened by him at all, but was very impressed by his speed and agility-he just zoomed up the sheer ice face and was gone. He didn't seem to be startled and fleeing, just moving on. It left me nonplussed for a few minutes, but eventually I resumed hiking. When I told our Sherpa guide about it, he said it was a yeti. Although his English was spotty, I got the impression there was a range of animals they considered to be a yeti, not just the Johnny Quest type abominable snowman we talk about over here. So whatever else is up there, at least in the early 1980s there were smallish apes with excellent climbing skills." B.F.

Chilling Hominid Encounter Recalled.

In the mid-1980, I was privy to an encounter that occurred not too far from State College, PA. A 19-year old local resident happened to be looking out his bedroom window which provided an excellent view of a pasture just west of his house. It was early morning (about 6:30 am local time) but there was plenty of light to see clearly. He was in the process of getting ready for work.

When he looked out the window, he noticed a tall, hairy creature walking in the pasture, coming from the north. The creature was taking long smooth strides and its arms moved back and forth as a human would. It did not appear to have a neck but capable of turning its head as it was constantly looking around. Except for the face, the creature was covered entirely with brown or black medium length hair. The witness was able to see the face and noticed that the forehead protruded distinctly. Also, it appeared the nose was wide and pushed close to the face. The height was approximately eight feet.

As the witness observed, the creature continued walking until it was south of the house. Suddenly, the creature stopped walking when the witness noticed two other similar creatures join it. Both were about one foot shorter than the first. At this point, one of the creatures reached down and picked up a piece of lumber that was part of a new shed being built. The larger creature started walking swiftly towards the house until it was within 50 feet of the residence. It stopped suddenly, made a few loud grunting sounds and glared toward the window from where the witness was watching.

The witness ducked and crawled to the far end of the bedroom. After a few minutes, the witness got up and looked out the window. The creatures were gone. Later that day, the witness and a friend discovered large unusual tracks in the pasture.

It's not known if this incident was ever reported but I do know that at least one local police officer knew what had happened and confirmed it with me. He seemed to be convinced that the witness was upstanding and honest but very private. The witness did move away from the area not long after the encounter fearing that the creatures would harm him.

[Note: this account was told to me several years ago by a woman who worked with the witness as well as the referenced police officer. I was in the area (Huntingdon, PA) investigating a haunting at the time and happened to come in contact with her. She did say that there were Bigfoot sightings before and after this incident. BFRO has a few sightings in surrounding counties listed though I don't know if these are related.]

Is Bigfoot An Extraterrestrial Being?

"I read your site daily and have enjoyed the personal stories by your readers. I had an experience when I was a boy that I hope would be of interest.

In September 1978, I lived with my father on a farm in the vicinity of Shawano, Wisconsin which is very near the Menominee Indian Reservation. There had been some buzz within the community of an unknown large hairy creature spotted by two deer hunters not far from our farm. I had heard stories of the Manabai'wok or 'The Giants' from stories told by the Menominee, but I just considered these tales to be legends.

Then one evening, my father and I were coming home from the store and noticed what appeared to be two hairy creatures collecting squash from the garden. Each creature was at least 6 foot tall. It was dusk but there was enough light to clearly see what they were doing. My father immediately cut the headlights and stopped the car as we just sat there and watched them pick and eat the squash. They didn't seem to even notice us even though we were about 100 feet from them. After about five minutes, one of the creatures looked in our direction and you could see its eyes glow red from the moonlight. We started to get scared and decided to make a dash for the house and call the police. Then suddenly, a huge disc-shaped object appeared above us and slowly moved towards the east field which was about 200 hundred yards from us and landed. I estimate the craft was about 40 feet in diameter. A large sliding door opened immediately and a foggy green light glowed from within the craft. After a few seconds, the door closed and craft slowly rose and shot off towards the north. Then we noticed that the creatures were gone.

A few days later, our neighbors from down the road came over for dinner. After we finished eating, my father and Mr. Cain walked outside. After an hour or so, the neighbors left and I started to clean up the kitchen. Later that evening, I was watching TV in the living room. My father walked in, turned off the TV and sat down beside me. He told me that Mr. Cain and his sister witnessed one of the craft on the same night that we had our encounter. As well, they witnessed several of the large hairy creatures meandering in the nearby woods. Mr. Cain said that he knew something had been in the woods for several weeks but never got a good look until the craft arrived. After that night, we never had another encounter or did we hear of more sightings by any people in the area.

Do you think that these creatures were Bigfoot, aliens or one in the same? It has always seemed strange to me that a Bigfoot body has never

been found. Is it a possibility that Bigfoot is an extraterrestrial being?"
Thanks, D.

Bigfoot Sighting - Northeast Frederick County, Maryland.

"I was on the way to the grocery store one day about 2-3 weeks ago and I saw something standing upright against or behind a tree. At least it looked that way. It happened when I was crossing a railroad track and that was against a hill that had a sharp bend at the top. So I didn't stop, fearing someone would come and hit me from behind. At the time I tried to tell myself that maybe it was a tree. So when I came back from the store whatever I saw wasn't there anymore and I just can't explain it."

It wasn't the same color as the tree. That's what made me curious. It was a light reddish brown with beige. Almost like the hair was 2-tone or something. The hair looked like it was in jagged tuffs that looked like it would look darker underneath if you lifted the fur. At the same time looked like you'd like to touch it (maybe that's because I'm a hairdresser). I can't explain what it was since I did not see a face nor did I see any arms and feet. But whatever it was, it was about 6 or 8 ft. tall from the ground to where it stopped about 6-8ft. alongside that tree. I did notice the part that I saw was a little rounded at the top as if suggesting a shoulder. It wasn't another tree since nothing else in the area (tree or bush) was that same color. I wish now that I gotten someone and looked for tracks. It has rained three or four times now so I guess I wouldn't be able to see anything. I may go look anyway. I don't know if it could have been a Sasquatch or what it could have been, but whatever it was it was standing straight and tall and didn't move."

I don't know if the ole big guy (if that's what he was) was passing by or he's a local? There have been sightings to the south of us (Little Bennett Campground in Frederick Co.) and some north of us in Adams County, Pa., which is just around 12-15 miles from here. I'd like to see him in the daylight again if that's what I saw. But it would scare me sh-less if I were to see him at night. I'm here by myself a lot at night and our dog wants to always go out. When she does, she acts like she is scared sometimes since she stays on the deck and looks. I sometime wonder what she is looking at. I know this may not be from your area, but thought you'd like to know. There may be others that come across your website as I have tonight with a similar story to tell from this same area. If so then maybe we have a local. Thanks for inviting me to tell my story. I just had the need to tell you because now you have this story for a reference in case someone else comes forward and tells you their story. I will definitely keep my eyes open and let you know if I notice anything else. I kind of got the feeling that these things (if that is what it was) are very adapted to blending into their surroundings. It actually looked like it would have been soft if I were able to touch it. People go out looking for Bigfoot all the time. They go places where they think they will see him, and all the time he's probably almost in their back yard. I have read that he will find you and now I believe that." Thanks, -*J.P.*

[Note: There have been several documented sightings in this general area over the years. The best known case involves 'The Dwayyo,' which is a canid-like hominid.]

Growing Up With Sasquatch, Marysville, Ohio.

"Hello, I saw the e-mail link at the bottom of your page and wanted to send these accounts to you. Though I've lived in Florida for just over 12 years now, I grew up in Ohio. I'm convinced that we had a Sasquatch that would pass through the area on a regular basis. This conviction is due to both sightings of it (them?) and other evidence. I had actually e-mailed Autumn Williams with these accounts several years ago after watching a few episodes of Mysterious Encounters when it was in production. She never bothered to write back in response, so I don't even know if she received the message. Since then, I contacted a researcher in Ohio with these events. Sorry to say, I don't recall the man's name. He was excited about it when he replied back to me with questions, but I've heard nothing since.

My parents and I moved into a house that was only a couple hundred yards from an abandoned railroad bed in Marysville, Ohio when I was 5-years-old. It wasn't long after that we, my friends and I, started our forays to the railroad bed. During the summer months, the weeds there would grow far taller than we were. For us, it was akin to being in a forest. Each summer, we'd carve a path through, using sticks to hack and slash at the weeds, cutting out a narrow, curving path and a larger open area where we'd gather to talk and whatnot.

When the Sasquatch first turned up, or, I should say, when we first noticed it, we were still young. We had no idea what was there. We felt that something was there on occasion, watching us. But for a long time we saw nothing. Then one of my friends reported having seen something large and hairy there one night. He saw it from a distance and only briefly. The rest of us didn't take him too seriously at first. He kept hounding us with it, though. Then another friend, a girl whose grandparents lived in the lot adjoining the railroad bed, saw something one night. She mostly lived with her grandparents due to family issues

30

and her bedroom window looked right out at the old railroad bed. Having a second report of something large and hairy up there at night made us all take it more seriously. Still, we were young and stupid. And the railroad bed was our place to go to get away from our parents. It was our place. We weren't going to give it up easily. Being so young still, we had no idea what we had. We started calling it a Troll. As we never had the impression that it was there full-time. So, we learned to live with it.

It's been suggested to me before, upon sharing these events, that the Sasquatch may have been young itself. I don't know. Several years went by. We were easing into our early teens. That's when things started to pick up. Maybe there was a juvenile. Maybe it was just watching us grow and decided that, while it was willing to allow young children to play there, it wasn't going to be so tolerant of older children. But the girl who lived right next to the railroad bed had several more night-time sightings. She was actually so afraid of what she saw that she convinced herself that she dreamed these, rather than truly admit that there was something there. I had three sightings of it/them over the years. She was with me for the first. We were in her grandparents' yard, walking up the short, gentle hill to the railroad bed. She froze and put her arm across my chest, stopping me. I looked at her. She was staring, open-mouthed and wide-eyed, pointing straight ahead. Through a narrow gap in the weeds, I saw what looked like the head and shoulders of a large humanoid figure with dark black hair. It was either sitting or crouched, holding perfectly still. We were seeing its profile. We backed slowly down the hill until it was out of sight, then turned and ran.

After that, she refused to ever go back up there. Not even as part of a group. The following day, we told another friend. He wanted to see the spot where the creature had been seen. It was broad daylight, so I took him up there, albeit reluctantly. The only sign we saw of it was a large patch of flattened grasses where it had been.

Somewhere in there, he and I also found what we referred to as the "vine cave," which I now believe to have been a nest. From our point of view, it simply popped into existence literally overnight in the large, open area we'd carved. He and I actually crawled into it a few times, but always felt very uncomfortable in it and always left quickly. Not long after the discovery of the "vine cave," a couple of rival kids destroyed it, thinking we'd built it. I think that may have well caused the increase in encounters with the Sasquatch and its attempts to chase us away.

My second and third sightings were spaced out over the next few years. Each time I saw it was in broad daylight. I was in our driveway, pulling weeds that were growing up through the gravel. Movement from

31

up at the railroad bed caught my attention. I looked up there to see a tall, humanoid being with long arms walking along the hill, moving to my right. It was covered in dark black hair. I've always suspected it was the same creature I saw on my first sighting, but don't know for sure. I watched it walk for a few seconds until it was blocked from view by a neighbor's storage shed. Then I turned and ran into the house. I didn't go back up to the railroad bed for weeks.

My third sighting was from a far greater distance. On the other side of the railroad bed was a fenced-in area of cow pasture and the local water tower. Beyond that was a trailer court. I was in our upstairs back bedroom one afternoon, again, during broad daylight. I saw what I first took to be a rolled-up rug by a trash can back in the trailer court. I could just barely see it, due to the distance. I looked away, and then looked back. What I was seeing seemed shorter, as if it had sagged, or crouched. I kept looking away, and then looked back, wanting to see if it moved. I couldn't tell if it was moving or not. Finally, I looked away for about ten minutes. When I looked back, whatever it had been was gone.

Another friend of mine lived in a house just beyond the far side of the trailer court. A wooden privacy fence divided his back yard from the trailer court. He once told me that he and his family would sometimes smell a heavy, musky scent at night. They would sometimes hear what sounded like heavy footfalls outside their house at night. He said his mother even claimed to have heard a loud heartbeat on occasion.

All in all, we were lucky. We gave it plenty of incentive to lash out at us. Luckily, it never did anything to hurt us. Just scare us, employing fear tactics. We were just too dumb and stubborn to pay close enough attention. Even after we'd all seen it.

Aside from the direct sightings of the creature(s), we had other evidence that it was there as well. Once, when I was in my teens and at the railroad bed alone, something that sounded very large was in the weeds and brush ahead of me, thrashing at the weeds, causing them to move and make a lot of noise. I thought at first it was the same friend who's wanted to go check out the site of my first direct sighting of the Sasquatch. About the same moment I realized that whatever was ahead of me was too large to be him a rock about the size of my fist was thrown at me, just narrowly missing hitting me in the head. I ran and refused to go back to the railroad bed for weeks after. Next time I was there alone I was in the same place and the same weed-thrashing occurred again. Luckily, no rock was thrown that time. Another time that same friend who wanted to see the spot of my first sighting and I were at the railroad bed by ourselves. There had to have been at the very least two of the creatures with us, one on either side of us. Nothing was thrown at us, but the same weed-thrashing noises started up to each side of us. Oddly, this time, nothing was moving that we could see. Both of us clearly heard the sounds, but couldn't see a thing moving. Still, after holding our ground for only a few moments, we both ran.

This same friend also decided to step up our own claims on the railroad bed after he had found a rock cairn built on our path one day. The cairn was small. My friend spouted his usual line of, "No f^*&ing monkey is going to chase me away!" and promptly kicked the cairn, scattered the stones. We gathered up new stones and built a new, larger cairn in place of the one we'd found. We left and went back the next day to find our own cairn scattered and a new, larger one in its place. My friend immediately kicked it apart and we built a new one, larger still, in place of the one we'd found. This went on for days; each day we'd find that the cairn we'd built the day before had been wrecked and new, larger, one would be in its place. Each day my friend would scatter the new one and we'd build our own, larger yet, in place of the most recent one we'd found. Secretly, I thought he was going back up to the railroad bed later and building the new cairn we would "find" the next day and he thought the same of me. Finally, after this had gone on long enough that the cairns were getting to be a bit larger than shoebox size, my friend decided to go one better and scent mark the cairn we'd just built. He told me what he was going to do and promptly unzipped his pants and urinated on the rock cairn we had just built. Afterward, we left and went to his house. We hung out on his front porch for two or three hours, talking, then decided to go check on the new, scent marked cairn. The smell hit us when we were still a good hundred yards, maybe more, from the cairn. We knew what we'd find and it scared both of us. As we'd been together for the entire intervening time, each knew that the other had not gone back to the railroad bed to do anything. The scent was an overpowering musk that was so strong it made us sick. Think skunk concentrate. We held our breath, ran in, saw what we knew we'd find, a new cairn that was noticeably larger than the one we'd built a few hours prior, and ran back out into clear air to breath. That stench lingered for days, but that ended the rock cairn war.

There were other times, before and after that, when my friends and I would be at the railroad bed and smell what smelled like a skunk. We also once found what looked to be shallow, crude pit toilets. We saw what looked to be finger marks in the mud and suspected they'd been dug out with very large bare hands. Several of the toilets contained what looked to be human fecal matter, only far larger.

The next door neighbors we had while I was growing up were very wasteful people. They didn't believe in leftovers from meals. If something wasn't eaten, it went into the trash, not the refrigerator. Their trash was torn open many, many times. They went to the expense of having a 5-foot-tall brick wall built around the area they kept their trash cans in. There was a green picket gate on the front for the garbage collectors to open to get access to the trash. They also bought trash cans with locking lids. None of it did any good. Whatever kept tearing into the trash would sometimes open the gate, leaving it open, and knew how to unlock the locked trashcan lids. I've often wondered if their trash wasn't why the Sasquatch liked that area and if it wasn't using the railroad bed as a convenient staging place to raid both their trash and trash from the aforementioned trailer court.

I have no evidence to support these claims. We were young and never thought to gather any evidence, something I kick myself for to this day. Having a Sasquatch passing though so closely so often didn't seem special to us because we were growing up with it.

The address for the house my parents and I lived in while all this went on is 623 East 6th Street, Marysville, Ohio 43040. We moved in when I was 5-years-old and moved out in 1998 when I was 22, only days before my 23rd birthday. Later I was told the railroad bed area has become even more abandoned and overgrown. But I've no idea if the Sasquatch is still there, or not." -S.H.

Gettysburg, PA Area Bigfoot Sighting.

I received a correspondence from a man in Indiana who wanted to remain anonymous. He and his family had spent the week vacationing in Gettysburg and were on their way home on a Friday night at around 8:30 pm. From the information I have gathered, he was driving westbound on US 30 (Lincoln Way-Chambersburg Rd) near the intersection of Rt. 234 (Buchanan Valley Rd) on the central eastern edge of Michaux State Forest, approximately 10 mile west of Gettysburg. He noticed that about 40 yards ahead of him a large, tall dark-haired humanoid darted out onto the highway (4 lanes wide) and bound across from north to south into the adjacent woods. He states that it seemed to take only 8-10 long strides in order to cover the width of the highway. He also states that the beast was carrying an object under its left arm but couldn't make out what it was. He said it looked towards him and he was able to get a look at the face which was lighter in color than the rest of the body. It was somewhat different than Bigfoot images he had remembered seeing, the face and chin were distinctively long.

The Return of the Boggy Creek Monster?

I received the following correspondence in reference to an encounter that occurred east of Texarkana, Arkansas. The sister of the witness (who lives in Florida) forwarded the account.

"Hello Sir, My brother and his wife had a shocking event on May 5th, 2011 when they were driving home to Genoa, Arkansas from a visit with his in-laws in Texarkana. He was driving east bound on Tennessee Rd (County Rd. 16) at around 7:30 pm and had just gone by Mosely Rd. when a creature suddenly jumped out of the trees and brush, crossed the road and blended into the thick woods. It was headed in the direction of Old Bitty Lake.

They both had a decent look at it and say it was about 6 foot tall and very stout with huge legs and feet. It was covered with very long reddish-brown hair that had dirt and debris stuck to it. When they stopped the car to look into the direction it went into the woods they got a whiff of a horrific stench (the windows were open).

I had heard the tales of the 'Fouke Monster' since I was a young girl but never bought into the hype. We actually lived near the Mercer Bayou at one point and talked to several people who verified the stories. My brother doesn't dare identity himself since he feels that it may cause problems but he felt there was a need for a warning.

I do believe him because he has never lied to me and is a very trustworthy, hard-working man. He is also a very experienced outdoorsman and knows the swamps and backwoods of southwest Arkansas liked the back of his hand. But this has left him shaken, to the point where he was at a loss for words when talking to me. That is VERY unlike him.

That's about all he had to say. Can you tell me of other sightings in the area?" Respectfully, -D

[Note: I've read many accounts about Arkansas swamp monsters over the years, none much different that this account. The area where this sighting supposedly occurred is only 10-15 miles north from the area of the 'Fouke Monster' incident. There have been many creatures and legends come from the swamps of Arkansas. The Fouke Monster is certainly one of the strangest. This six-feet-tall, hairy, humanoid monster gained notoriety in the late 1960's when it harassed two families living outside this town in the southwest part of the state. The monster is reported to have smelled awful and made a habit of killing chickens and livestock and mauling a number of dogs. The story became so popular that a low-budget horror movie titled *The Legend of Boggy Creek* was made about it in 1973.]

Bigfoot Duo Reported at Nelson Lake, Wisconsin.

I received this email from a young man in Sawyer County, Wisconsin who claims to have witnessed two Bigfoot, an adult and juvenile, while fishing:

"Sir, I am writing about a sighting I had on June 26th around 8:00 pm at Nelson Lake, Wisconsin. I was fishing from my canoe about 30yds from the shore near Tanning Point when I noticed a whimpering sound. It was coming from the woods at the shoreline. It sounded like a dog whining, so I stopped what I was doing to watch the woods to see if anything appeared. After a few seconds I saw a child scampering from the woods. I didn't get a very good look but the child had very thick brown hair all over its body and was very small (human toddler size). It quickly showed itself then bolted back towards the woods.

I sat there in shock. But within seconds I heard three distinct and angry 'grunts.' I then saw a large ape-like head rise above the lower tree boughs. The eyes were barely visible but I could tell that it didn't want me there. That was enough for me so I started to paddle towards the north shore when all of a sudden I heard a loud 'plop' then 'splash' from behind the boat. I turned around in time to see another rock heading in my direction. It was many yards away from me but I got the message.

I was shaking from the time I witnessed these beasts up until a few hours later when I was in my home office pondering what I had seen. I think it may have been Bigfoot. I Googled 'Wisconsin Bigfoot' and your blog came up. Was this a Bigfoot? I'm not an outdoorsman though I enjoy canoeing and fishing. Have there been other sightings in this area? Is there a danger? I appreciate your help.

I am a state employee so I would prefer my identity remain confidential. Thank you."

Possible Bigfoot Detected, Yadkin River, Davie County, NC.

I received the following inquiry from a witness seeking an explanation:

"I live in west-central North Carolina. I live at a location that is very close to the Yadkin River in Davie County. The river's flood plain comes to my property line in a valley with no houses and heavily wooded, however two roads to cross to get to my house. The river's edge is primarily undeveloped, with almost a 300 yard flood area clearance on both sides for miles and miles. This river floods regularly, but not very much lately. There are high voltage power lines running across the area as well. Now that the stage is set, let's go. We have also put a game camera out to see if we could catch anything on is. We so far have caught a fat pregnant deer, several raccoons and a grey fox. That pregnant deer has twins now have been in our garden. The deer are pretty thick around here.

This is not a hot bed of Bigfoot sightings. But I have been hearing something very large walking in the woods beside my house. My dog has been kicked by something and knocked out for a few seconds. All we heard that night was a thud as it sounded like he was kicked in the side. We saw nothing as it was around 11:30 p.m. on a moonless night. A few moments later, he was up chasing a scent down the neighbor's field. My son grabbed his flashlight and looked around down at the wood line and caught a pair of large red-orange eyes reflection. We went down later to investigate where they were. There is an opening right where he saw the eyes. We determined that whatever it was had to stand about four feet tall or so if it was standing in the field and nine feet tall if it was standing in the woods as the opening has a steep drop off to the tree he used as a reference spot. The last explanation is that whatever it is was in the tree at that level. We are hunters and spend time in the woods often. We have never seen a pair of red-orange eyes around here. Not sure what a bear's eyes look like, but we have no bear population around here.

I often stay up very late and go outside to look around with the flashlight around 3 or 4 in the morning. I have heard on three occasions a very loud knock following my spotlighting around. It sounds like two large rocks being hit together, not like a rock hitting a tree. They have come from three different spots down in the back yard in the woods. The knock sounds are only heard about once every 8-12 days. Kind of like whatever it is only passes through this area on some kind of schedule. Not sure if that sounds logical? I have only on one occasion heard what I would call a howl. It was in the distance and was NOT a coyote. Not even close. It was a different tone and lasted too long.

"I would love to hear a logical explanation for all of this." -K.

This is a follow up to the above post. I received two emails that referenced 'something' stalking the same general area. Both witnesses requested to remain anonymous.

"Concerning the 'Bigfoot on the Yadkin River in Davie County' story. I live several miles up-river from where this event took place. I am approximately four miles from the Yadkin River but at night on occasion I have heard the tree knocking, the howls but I have never seen one or saw a track. I have a tendency to stay out of the woods at night in the summertime due to copperheads and Poison Ivy.

When I first started hearing the howls it happened on a regular basis from about 10:00 p.m. to 1:00 a.m. or 2:00 a.m. At first I thought it could have been some type of owl but that didn't match up. One day I was looking at an investigation that had been done in upstate New York when they started to play the howling sounds that had been recorded from a possible Bigfoot encounter and it was exactly like I heard. My dogs also have been at times seriously pissed at something in the woods across the road from my house and keeping them from going after it is almost impossible.

Please do not reveal my name or contact info if you publish this letter. The next time I hear the sounds I will post it on here if you would like for me to. Best regards."

I received another email the next day.

"I read your piece about an unknown animal or possible Bigfoot in Davie County. I live between Advance, NC and the Yadkin River and I can say that I have experienced related noises that include wood knocking and weird howls. I also caught a glimpse of a large man-like beast in the Eureka Mills area last fall while canoeing. This thing rose up from the brush in a clearing. I was about 50ft. from the bank and it was another 50ft off the shore. It dashed off so quick I barely saw it, but I know it wasn't a deer, bear or human.

I have heard stories of sightings but people around here kind of keep these things quiet. One of my friend's neighbors down the road from me had a heavy metal sliding door ripped off his barn a few months ago. He said that one of his goats was carried off also. He called the local police who came out and saw large footprints in the mud. That incident never made any news. There is something moving up and down the river as far as I'm concerned. Good luck"

I received several inquiries from investigators since I posted the original email. The only information I can forward is what I have posted so far. I am not going to release any names or specifics without consent by the witnesses.

Bigfoot Burial Ritual?

The following email was quite strange and needs further investigation. The email was written as a draft including an outline that was added with other notations. It was an odd format, but the information was verified. I was asked by the submitter (DD) to write the commentary since they felt that they were not able to compose a story that would be understood by the readers.

I forwarded a copy of my final composition to DD which was approved. I inquired about the witness' (the cousin) willingness to be interviewed but that notation was rebuffed since the information sent to me was done so without the knowledge of the witness. All specific personal and location disclosure was agreed to be kept in confidence. Here is the transcript:

"During the recent holidays I was able to talk to a cousin who lives in the Pharaoh Lake area in New York. He is a conservationist and an advocate for nature. He recently made a discovery that is fascinating but pains him since the information would most likely lead to Bigfoot hunters decimating wildlife and pristine forests. While hiking and camping in a fairly remote forest in Essex County, NY (the most specific location he will give) he came across what he describes as a "Bigfoot ritual burial."

One evening while he was making his way back to camp he heard "muffled grunting" coming from his right. His attention was directed toward a thick stand of sugar maple trees. He crouched down behind a large fallen tree and witnessed three large hairy bipedal figures, Bigfoot standing around a large tree stump. It looked like a large female who towered above her companions. He estimated that she was 8 foot+ and that the others were about 5-6 feet tall. Each one of the figures was "swaying' and "grunting." This activity continued for almost 10 minutes when they suddenly stopped and started to run in the opposite direction. He was fearful that they had noticed his presence somehow. Since it was now getting dark he decided to continue to his camp and return the next day.

The next morning he anxiously made his way back to the site where he had seen the Bigfoot. When he reached the site he noticed a 4 foot high hollow sugar maple stump with four gray squirrel tails attached to the top edge and suspended outside the stump. It looked like a "sort of decoration." He also noticed a terrible stench that reminded him of very strong urine. He looked into the stump - it was empty, but there was some dark fur, a few blood stains and a large piece of old deer hide.

39

He surmises that the Bigfoot "buried" a small child or infant in the stump and that they either came back to move it after noticing him or that a scavenger took it during night.

Do you or others believe that this could have been a Bigfoot 'funeral' or ritual burial?" -DD

Bigfoot Pair Encountered Near Crane Lake, Minnesota.

"Hello Sir, I am writing you about an incident my daughter and I had this past weekend near Crane Lake, Minnesota. We were on our way home and traveling south on Crane Lake Road only a few miles from the lodge we had stayed the weekend. As we drove around a wide bend in the road we noticed two tall dark creatures walk out of the forest to my left. I slammed the brakes and stopped about 30 feet from them. They seemed oblivious to us as they walked onto the road and barely gave us a glance. They crossed in front of the car and leaped over a ditch then into the forest. I quickly hit the gas pedal and drove for about a quarter mile. I then pulled over to collect myself. My daughter, who is 15, was sitting with a shocked look and not moving. My heart was racing and I was shaking uncontrollably.

I think we sat there without saying a word to each other for over a minute. I then asked my daughter what she thought those creatures were. Immediately she said that we had seen 'Bigfoot.'

Both creatures were about seven foot tall and massively built. I was surprised by the amount of dark reddish hair they both had and how proportionate their bodies were to humans. I saw the face of one of the creatures briefly as it glanced at us. The nose was very broad but the rest of the face was similar to those you see on TV that are supposed to be cavemen. They walked upright like humans and didn't slouch. I believe they were both male.

I have lived in Minnesota (in St. Cloud) all my life and I never heard of anyone seeing a 'Bigfoot.' My daughter is convinced that these creatures were 'Bigfoot.' We looked online and found your website and an image that best represents what we witnessed.

Have there been sightings in the Crane Lake area previously? I called the lodge where we stayed and the woman who answered said that there had been a few sightings in the area over the years but nothing that close to their location. I'd be interested to know what it was we saw. I can't believe that there are not more reports of these creatures. Thanks for reading." -*MM*.

[Note: I posted the email as I received it. I contacted the witness by an alternate email she provided, she replied that I could post her report minus any personal information. She added that her daughter has had nightmares since the encounter and that they have not mentioned the incident to anyone else other than the woman at the lodge. I told the witness that these encounters are something that you never forget (from personal knowledge). I sincerely hope her daughter's nightmares subside, though I have known of some witnesses who suffer PTSD long after these close encounters. I didn't get a time but they had just checked out so I assume it was during daylight on Monday morning.]

I also contacted the lodge where MM and her daughter stayed this past weekend. I talked to a very nice lady who asked me to talk to someone who knew the area better than her. Another woman got on the telephone and asked me to call her back at another number. Well, we played 'phone tag' for most of the afternoon (seems like it's busy at the lodge) but finally she was able to talk.

I inquired about Bigfoot sightings in the area. She said that there had been several reports north of their location in Ontario's Quetico Provincial Park and that there had been an expedition (I supposed it was BFRO) near Voyageurs National Park in the summer of 2011. She said several of the people in the expedition party had stayed at their lodge. I gave her my contact number / email and asked that she contact me if other information became available.

The Dark Walker.

I received the following correspondence a few days ago. It was forwarded by 'John' a retired Federal employee who lives in northern Nevada and who wishes to remain anonymous. The story centers around an experience John had while living with his Grandfather. John later stated that the property was in a rural area of Aleppo Township in Greene County, Pennsylvania. He did not want to pinpoint the location but did say that he wanted the anecdote dedicated to his Grandfather, Samuel Hill, who he considers the most remarkable man he has ever known.

John seemed quite sincere in my opinion. He decided to come forth with the account after he had a rather strange encounter a few months ago (which he did not want to discuss). John did mention in his most recent email that he was 81 years old and a veteran of the Korean War.

41

He also stated that he truly felt his Grandfather's actions were taken in defense of his family:

"When I was a boy my mother and I lived with my grandfather who had a farmhouse in a rural location in southwestern Pennsylvania. My grandfather was a handyman who also worked a small blacksmith shop in his old barn. My grandmother had died before I was born and my father had also passed away while serving overseas in the U.S. Army.

Beginning in the summer of 1946, we noticed strange howling sounds coming from the woods that surrounded the property. The activity came at night and was very frightening when the howling came close. The sounds didn't seem to bother my grandfather though my mother and I were shaken when it would begin. The sounds continued off and on for about a year but we never noticed any animals. My grandfather and I would hunt for deer and squirrel in the woods during the colder months but we never saw signs of unusual animal activity.

One late afternoon in the spring of 1947, I was helping my grandfather in his shop when I noticed something moving around the edge of the woods near an area where by grandfather had a few junk cars and other items. It was about 200 feet from our location but I clearly noticed someone or something moving around. I told my grandfather to look. He walked to the door, lit his pipe and said nothing. After a minute or two he turned around and got back to work. About that time this thing moved into the woods and disappeared. I couldn't judge how big it was but it sort of reminded me of a magazine picture I had seen of a large ape that was said to inhabit in the Asian jungles.

Later that evening I told my mother what I had seen. She was shocked because she knew I wouldn't lie to her and that the howling sounds had been closer lately. I also told her of my grandfather's response when I pointed the creature out to him. She immediately stood up and walked into the sitting room in order to ask my grandfather what it was. He started to shake his head slowly and said that he was hoping that we wouldn't 'see it' because he was worried we would be scared and leave him.

After assuring him that we'd never leave him my mother again insisted that he tell us what this creature was. He looked away, took a deep breath and said 'it's a Dark Walker' and said that it had lived in the woods for many years. He said the native Indians called it 'Stone Spirit' and they thought that it was an evil spirit who would appear when someone was about to die. The last time he had seen the 'Dark Walker' was the night before my grandmother died. My mother was skeptical of

42

the 'harbinger of death' angle but she sensed that there was something unnatural nearby.

The howling continued each night though we hadn't seen any signs of the 'Dark Walker.' One warm evening we were sitting on the back porch. There were a few howls but it seemed like the sounds were further away. We were listening to the radio when all at once my grandfather stood up and looked out towards the barn. He turned to me and said 'John, go get my pistol and ammo, hurry now.' I ran into the sitting room and grabbed the .455 Webley revolver and a handful of bullets from the old steamer trunk. I handed it to him and watched him load the gun. He then picked up a hatchet and slid it in his pants belt. 'Now both of you get into the house, now!' We were in the kitchen looking through the screen door and watched my grandfather walk slowly towards the barn. We saw him turn and walk out of sight into the dark. I decided to grab my shotgun and keep it nearby. After a minute or so we heard three gunshots and a blood curdling scream emanate from the woods near the barn. Then it suddenly stopped and there was complete quiet. We were frozen and wondering if we should go look for my grandfather. A few seconds later we heard him yell 'stay in the house until I come back.'

I heard the pickup truck start up. I looked out the storage room window and saw my grandfather drive to the back of the barn and park. Several minutes later he backed up and drove by the side of the house out onto the road. I could see that there was something in the back covered up with a tarp. It was getting late so my mother told me to go to bed.

The next morning I came downstairs and sat beside my grandfather who was reading the newspaper and drinking a cup of coffee. My mother was sitting at the other end of the table staring at my grandfather. Not long later she said 'well dad, tell him.' My grandfather put the paper down and looked at me. 'I killed the Dark Walker.' That was all he said. My mother told me not to tell anyone and that the matter was closed.

We never talked about it again. My grandfather lived another 15 years and my mother stayed with him until his dying day. When I grew older I moved away and raised a family. I would return home to visit each summer, and never heard another howl. John

I asked John if he thought the 'Dark Walker' was a Bigfoot or hominid. He responded by stating that he didn't think it was a hairy man or human-like creature. He thought it seemed more animal-like than human and that it moved lower to the ground, at least during the brief time he observed it. John mentioned that there were Shawnee legends of similar creatures but he never found a reference to a 'Stone Spirit.' For the time being, I'm going to consider this a hominid encounter.

Chapter 3

In early autumn 1988 I was at a local exhibition near Baltimore and bumped into Andy, an old friend who was there as part of a group from the Boy Scouts of York-Adams Area Council (Pa.). Both of us had been Boy Scouts together and I was happy to see that he continued as a troop leader. We decided to grab a bite to eat and catch up a bit, it had been 12 years since we had seen each other. After a while, the subject of my paranormal investigations came into the conversation. He had always been fascinated with ghost sightings at Gettysburg and the surrounding area and had camped near the battlefield on several occasions.

Andy stated that a few of the local troops had recently been camping at the old Camp Conewago and some of the boys had reported hearing "crying" sounds and were spooked bad enough that a few left their campsites early. They had setup their campsites deeper than usual in the woods near the Conewago Creek fork (where the Little Conewago and main Conewago Creek meet). He stated that he and another scout leader were going to check out the area the following weekend and he wanted to know if I'd at least go up for the day and investigate with them. I accepted the invitation.

Camp Conewago is located north of New Oxford, Pa. in Adams County along the main Conewago Creek upstream from Dick's Dam. It was established in 1919 for exclusive use by the local Boy Scouts of America. The area is rich in early colonial history since it was located on a major hunting route used by the Susquehannock Indians. Several attempts to establish settlements in this area failed because of Indian raids. As well, the Susquehannocks constantly warred with neighboring tribes. The Susquehannocks were eventually forced back into northeast Maryland and Delaware and the colonists were able to expand westward into the Allegheny Mountains. The area became an important trading stop for settlers to stock up on supplies and to get updates before heading into the wilderness.

I met with Andy and John the following Friday at the campground. I was shocked at how little the place had changed. A flood of boyhood memories came over me while I walked around the cabins and the administration building. Andy wanted to know how long I planned to stay and that they were going to setup camp in the same area of the reports. I was game, so I told him I'd stay for the weekend, grabbed my gear and followed them into the woods. I suppose we hiked about 500 yards or so before we came to the bank of the creek, then we followed the creek for another 300 yards until we came to the fork. We setup 3 tents and had a nice fire going in short order. It was around 7:00 pm by this time, so we decided stay close to camp for the remainder of the evening.

The first night was fairly uneventful, though I sensed that something was watching us. I didn't say anything but kept my eyes open and head clear. These woods are somewhat thick with ground cover and are inhabited by a fair amount of wildlife, especially white-tailed deer and raccoons. I remember when I was a Boy Scout, the older kids would send out the new members of the scout troop on an initiation "snipe" hunt. They'd give the prospective "hunter" a burlap bag and a flashlight and set them out into the woods at night telling them they could return only after they caught a "snipe." They were usually running back to the campsite within an hour scared to the point of tears. It was a bit cruel, but we all had to go through the indignity, it was a tradition.

The next morning was sunny and cool, a perfect day to explore the woods. We sat down to breakfast when John asked if we heard footsteps and movement during the night. Andy said he slept straight through the night. I said I heard some movement but assumed it was one of my companions. Nothing seemed to be disturbed in the campsite, so we dismissed it, though I still had this lingering sense that we were being watched. We spent the day walking for several miles through the woods and examining points of interest. I wasn't picking up any spirit connections and started to think that this was going to be a quiet weekend. About 6:00 pm we got back to camp and sat down to talk about any little thing that came into our heads.

Later that evening, we were sitting around the fire engaged in a conversation about football when suddenly a scream rang out west and upstream from our location. I thought it sounded like an owl at first, but a few minutes later it happened again and it distinctively sounded like a child. I couldn't tell how far away it was but it lasted for several seconds and seemed to fade in and out. We got up and walked a few yards into the woods expecting to hear the sound again. It was quiet for about an hour and we were discussing what could have naturally caused that sound. I have heard bobcats, owls and rabbits scream and none sounded close to this. We agreed that it was definitely the cries of a child.

We decided to stay up for the entire night. There was a full moon and much of the woods and creek were visible. At approximately 1:00 am, I was walking the perimeter of our camp when I suddenly felt like

46

something was watching me. I stood still and tried to gauge what was going on. I told Andy and John what I felt and we started to walk deeper into the woods towards the fork. We walked about 50 feet when, without warning, we recognized to our right a large dark figure with bright red eyes standing in the creek, and suddenly it shot straight up into the air with an audible "whoosh." A few seconds later, we heard another scream that seemed to fade as if was moving away from us.

We hurried back to the campsite and compared thoughts about this phantom. Andy was shook up and didn't talk for several minutes until I prodded him for his recollection. John was surprising calm and estimated that it was six foot or so, dark in color and seemed to have something extending from its back. I also noticed the structures on the back and commented that it reminded me of wings but I was unsure. We all agreed that it had bright red eyes. This creature or phantom jettisoned so fast that we didn't even have time to get a flashlight on it. Andy wanted to spend the night in the administration building and come back and collect our gear in the morning. He and John walked back, but I decided to stay in the campsite for the remainder of the night. Nothing significant occurred though that feeling of being watched remained.

After the investigation and further research, I concluded that this creature or phantom was more than a simple spirit or energy. I was aware of the numerous sightings of a "Mothman" in West Virginia and it seemed that this being was somewhat similar in description, but I have significant doubt that it is a cryptid [Note: I have since changed my mind.] I and other researchers have investigated this area since our sighting and have come up with minimal evidence, though a report of a dark creature was made by a resident who lived near Dick's Dam a few years later. The investigation remains open, hopefully I or someone else will be able to offer a plausible answer in the future.

In 2008, I received an email from a man who lived a mile or so downstream from this incident (near Dick's Dam). He stated that he had heard similar screams for many years and that the frightful sounds continued to this day. A scout leader also emailed me approximately the same time and wanted to tell me that a few of the boys in his troop had witnessed what they described as a 'dragon' that was 6 foot tall with wings and a tail, but looked like it had fur or feathers. He said that the boys seemed serious but thought they were 'showing off' and dismissed their claims until later when he read the account of my experience.

Since that time, I have continued to check up on the area to see if anything strange develops. The Native American folklore and stories from settlers who inhabited the area offer several possibilities as to the

47

identity of this cryptid but to date, I have not been able to make a plausible theory as to what is being heard or seen.

The Next Sighting of the Conewago Phantom.

I just received an email in May 2011 in reference to another winged humanoid sighting in northeast Adams County, PA:

"Sir, on Sunday, May 8th at dusk I was traveling east on Hunterstown Rd. Rt. 394 towards Hampton, PA. Just before I started to cross Conewago Creek I plainly saw a large creature with wings fly over the bridge in front of me. It was about 100 ft. in front of the car. The creature was dark in color and was as big as a full grown adult human. I looked in the direction in which it flew but I lost sight of it. I asked a neighbor (I live in Hampton) if she had ever heard of anything like this. She said there was a rumor of a sighting near the Boy Scout camp a few years ago. I searched the internet and found your story including the second sighting near Dick's Dam. Have you determined what this thing is? Is there a chance that it could hurt anyone?" -E.

There was another sighting reported at Camp Conewago in 2008 but a specific location was not determined. There had been four reported sightings in an approximate eight square mile area to date.

Was it the 'Conewago Phantom?'

I received another inquiry on June 1, 2012:

"I saw a flying 'something' during the evening of April 29th around 7:50 pm as I was driving north on Harmony Grove, Rd near the Conewago Creek crossing. I noticed something fly straight up into the air from behind the trees on the creek bank. It shot straight up just at tree top and spread its wings and flew east towards Pinchot State Park. It was not a bird, just too big. I don't know what it was but I'd say it was about 10ft high and had wings like a bat. I didn't notice a head or tail. It was black in color. No feathers. I searched Google and your story came up. I didn't know about the Conewago Phantom sightings. I don't know if it was that thing. I did find something like a large bird seen north of York back in 2006. I found some photos on Google Maps of where this thing was seen by me. Any idea what it was? Thanks" -J.S., Dover, PA

The witness had scant information to add to the original email other than he was sure that this was not a bird. He mentioned that it was a bit overcast but he thought he got a better contrast of the creature because of that. I'm starting to wonder if the increased numbers of large bird-like creature sightings reported throughout Pennsylvania are connected somehow.

Are 'Mothman' and the 'Conewago Phantom' Parallel Beings?

On June 28, 2012, I received an email from another witness in reference to a possible sighting of the 'Conewago Phantom' approximately 1 mile downstream from the most recent report from April 29th. He also mentions another possible sighting nearby on Rt. 74 just north of Dover, PA:

"Sir, my girlfriend was driving over to spend the night at my home after she had gotten off work (2nd shift) had seen a "very large bird" the size of a car fly in front of her as she was driving south on route 74 crossing the Conewago Creek bridge in York County, PA at around 1:30am about three weeks ago.

Odd that we had also seen a very broad shouldered tall man walking east in the bright moonlight (remember that bright moonlight night a month or two ago?) through a farmer's field adjacent to the Lighthouse Baptist Church at 12:30 am just several weeks prior." -M.M.

As of September 22, 2012 this was the most recent reported sighting of the 'Conewago Phantom.' All of the sightings were adjacent to the Conewago Creek on a stretch of approximately 4 miles. All the witnesses were forthcoming to me though, each was reluctant to have their name mentioned in the report. I grew up in the general area and know intimately that these witnesses would likely face harsh ridicule. So far the local press has been reluctant to report the sighting, which is fine with me, simply because I don't want to be chasing false reports.

The 'Conewago Phantom' is likely related to the birdman-type entities that will be described in the next chapter. Since I was an eyewitness to this cryptid it's obvious to me that it parallels the infamous Mothman.

Chapter 4

Mothman.

Mothman is a legendary creature reportedly seen in the Point Pleasant area of West Virginia from November 15, 1966 to December 15, 1967. The first newspaper report was published in the Point Pleasant Register dated November 16, 1966, entitled "Couples See Man-Sized Bird...Creature...Something." Mothman was said to be related to a wide array of supernatural events in the area, including the deadly collapse of the Silver Bridge on December 15, 1967. Since that time, the Mothman has been called a harbinger of death and destruction and has been reportedly seen worldwide.

Many of the reports that I have received over the years are concentrated in the Ohio River Valley, from southeast Ohio, through West Virginia and into northern Kentucky; but there are other sightings worldwide. I have also included several varied flying humanoid reports.

Tall Dark 'Mothman' Type Entity Reported, Stow, Ohio.

The Munroe Falls Paranormal Society contacted me in reference to this sighting (unedited):
"MFPS was contacted by a person who had an extremely odd sighting of an entity here in Stow, OH an adjacent community of my hometown. Witness' wife contacted me with story and after several days of negotiation, witness agreed to meet with me, recreate the events and answer questions. Witness extremely hesitant, but wife persuaded him to give story. Night of 9/14/09 witness, who wishes to remain anonymous, but name and other vitals on record, was driving to work, 10:15pm, Northbound on Hudson Drive. As witness drove under the RT8 overpass bridge, just north of the Hudson Drive Applebee's Restaurant, he witnessed a 9-10' tall solid black entity standing on the southbound side of the road. No discernible head or facial features noticed. Duration approx. 5-10 secs. Distance approx 15-20' from his vehicle.

Witness had the feeling the entity was watching him and was "there" for him only. No other vehicles/persons present during sighting. Immediately after turning his head back to the road, he looked in rearview mirror, entity no longer visible. Did not see entity depart or disappear. Witness became extremely upset and scared. Felt that he paled, and his eyes began to water uncontrollably. First thought was to turn around and go home, calling off of work. He tried to call his wife at home, but cell phone would not work, either from the programmed address book, or manual input calling. Kept getting "call failed," which has never happened before. Cell phone continued to be affected all the way to the I-271 entrance ramp, approx. 8-10 miles up the road. Witness did make it to his job, but has since regretted not turning around and going home, due to his state of mind. The experience was traumatic in every sense of that word. It was a "bad" night for him at work.

Weather was clear, starry. No other known witnesses, no animal sightings. Other than the uncontrollable watering of the eyes, no other physiological or physical effects on his person. Other than the cell phone not working, no other effects noticed on inanimate objects, such as streetlights, car, or timepiece (watch). There was no religious interpretation, no known memory lapse, no dreaming related to sighting as of this report. Witness did report close encounter with UAO as a ten year old when he lived in Akron, other than that, no overt paranormal experiences were reported during his normal daily life. Witness tried to box his sighting into something prosaic. Closest he could come was an electric company canvas transformer covering, but on reflection, he's certain that that was not what he observed. Entity too tall, too big for that. Witness stated that immediately after the sighting he became more and more agitated and scared the further he drove along. Distinct feeling that the entity was waiting for him and possibly following him, but he did not see it again, that night. No disturbances at witness place of residence. The following day on his way home, as he neared the RT8 overpass, this time driving over the bridge he went under the day before, as he approached the bridge area, his eyes began to water uncontrollably once again, as he drove over the bridge and his eyes continued to water, until he passed beyond the bridge, then his eyes began to clear up.

Witness provided me a pencil drawing of what he observed. When I first saw the drawing I was incredulous. The drawing bears an uncanny resemblance to the original drawing submitted by the original Mothman witness of Point Pleasant WV, 1966. Witness willing to keep me informed of any further sightings or activity. I believe I have gained his trust, as I mentioned he wasn't really interested in coming forth with this. My intuitive reaction is that witness is extremely believable and honest in his testimony. No outrageous embellishments to either his story, which I made him relate twice, nor to his drawing, which was really rather simple in nature.

So in the end, no answers at this point, but the eerie drawing he provided and its uncanny resemblance to the Mothman legacy are very much intriguing. I will continue to correspond and follow up with witness periodically and will be anxiously waiting to see if any other sightings are reported in this vicinity that might validate this entity's appearance."

Human Adult-Sized Flying Cryptid - Pacific, Missouri.

"We were in Pacific, MO, tonight around 11:30 PM and noticed a massive flying creature, not once but three times. My son even noticed it on his own the third time. We were near a large cliff/mountain with some type of cave openings. We don't live in the area, I can say for sure we turned onto a road called Viaduct Road, went past a fire station and continued on for about 1 mile before we first noticed it. It was brownish/grey and the body portion was at least the size of a large adult human. This creature was tracking us - in a circle pattern. We were driving an Escalade with the blue color headlights and this may have cause interest in us. The third time around we viewed it in front of the vehicle, around the driver side and around towards the rear of the vehicle. The factory tinted windows did help it vanish into the sky from our point of view.

Please understand when we could see it the range must have been about 150 feet in the air, not more than 250 feet. The distance was never less than 100 yards, often much greater. We were going about 35- 45 MPH. I have never thought of anything like this in my life! It is 3:33 AM and my son and I are wide awake in a hotel, 17 miles away from the place we first noticed the creature. Please notify me if you become aware of similar sightings. Thanks."

Flying Humanoid, Borne Sulinowo, Poland.

I received the report from a reader in Poland (unedited):

"Sir, I report to you from Poland. On a particular day in April 2008, Mrs. Izydora from Szczecinek, northern Poland went with her husband on a trip to Borne Sulinowo area. The man parked their car and soon they departed. While her husband went toward the local forest, Mrs. Izydora decided to stroll amongst ruins of the local military base. It was about 1-2 p.m.

Suddenly woman felt strange but decided to walk further. After a while she unexpectedly noticed in the mid-air some kind of semi-transparent entity. As she said, it looked like a 'misty figure' of a man hovering several meters above the ground. Mrs. Izydora could see its exact shape since the silhouette was outlined by whitish contour making it quite noticeable.

For some time the witness remained as if paralyzed and unable to scream while the being was hovering nearly directly above her. It remained in the air in a distance of a few meters and kept its arms stretched 'as if preparing to flight.' After a while of observation woman decided to retreat to her car parked nearby.

The scared woman began her retreat to the car, but then she noticed that the being started to follow her and rapidly flew above disappearing in the nearby woods. Then woman called her husband and forced him to leave the place immediately. She told him about the weird incident two days later.

Woman used a word 'male' in description of the being's appearance. As she told the being despite the lack of distinctive details of appearance had a solid and massive shape, resembling a tall man. It moved smoothly and without any sound. Mrs. Izydora said that the being seemed to be 'misty' with a distinct outline.

The whole observation lasted a few minutes but Mrs. Izydora couldn't recall it exactly. Another interesting fact is some kind of possible influence of the witness physical condition. Mrs. Izydora felt weak but it isn't clear if it was connected with the being appearance. The other feeling was paralysis which prevented her from calling husband. A strange feeling passed away as soon as being disappeared in the woods.

As it is mentioned above Mrs. Izydora decided to talk about the incident after a few days. We talked to her after more than half a year after the encounter and she still was frightened. She told us that she never expected to experience such an encounter with something she could not explain rationally. Beside Mrs. Izydora is open-minded person she doesn't want to come back to that place despite the fact that previously it was often visited by her and her husband."

Mothman Sighting near Cincinnati, Ohio.

I received an email in reference to incidents experienced by the witness and her friend. The location was near Cincinnati, Ohio (unedited):

"It was about 8:00 pm and I was driving home after dropping a friend off at her house. I came to an intersection, a red light, and stopped. Nothing out of the normal, just a regular night. The roads were fairly deserted. While waiting for the light to change I saw something that looked like the back end of a deer as it quickly crossed the street. I didn't think much of it except for the fact that when I drive through there I have to be careful because deer apparently like to jump in front of cars. That stretch of road is only a couple hundred feet posted at 40 mph. I slowed to about 30-35 mph to watch and look at the deer.

When I looked to see if the deer was still there I witnessed something quite a bit different. This massive thing was standing back a ways but it was clearly visible. The yard it was standing in has a huge white shed with a light attached to the front though; this didn't help because it cast a big shadow. The figure stood on the ground but its height reached to about the top of the doors to the shed. It had two curved like masses coming from the sides. But the most obvious feature were the deep red, glowing eyes coming from the center of the black mass. It was something I couldn't stop looking at. I continued to drive but all the way home I felt I was being followed." -L.

I later received the following from the previous witness:

"I'd like to share an experience my friend and I have unfortunately been dragged into. At approximately 10:30 PM tonight, I received an instant message from my friend about a rather disturbing encounter she had. She had reported she saw the Mothman. I sent her several messages back, asking if she was alright, if she was there, etc. She eventually sent me a text message with a picture that she drew of the creature attached. By this point, I was literally getting sick and trembling due to anxiety and fright. We began talking about it and I noticed a tapping at my window; a very light kind of sound. My dogs both jerked their heads upward and stared at the window for a long time. Being in the state I was in, I refused to look.

For a while, the tapping stopped, she and I continued to discuss the matter at hand. Suddenly, the tapping began again, but this time the dogs ignored it and so did I. About four or five minutes later, I fought the urge to stare at my computer monitor and looked at my window. My blinds were closed, but I could faintly see something red and glowing, like taillights that had somehow made their way into the neighbor's backyard. I quickly looked away, not wanting to see it anymore. I looked again a couple minutes later, unnerved to see the red glow was still there. Again, I looked away and continued discussing this with my friend. Finally, I turned my head one final time and saw that the glow no longer remained.

As I'm typing this email, I'm really worried, as the tapping has begun again and I'm really too afraid to move from this position. Above this, I've included my friend's side of the story, and, should you post this, we would certainly appreciate if you could put them both into one piece. We'd discussed calling the police, but she didn't want to make a big deal about it. Her parents brushed it off and I have yet to tell anyone in my house about this.

I'm not sure what this was; a frightening delusion or a real situation, but I'm not sure if I'm willing to face the facts and find out. Thanks for your time. -A. (This was sent to the *Mothman Museum* as well)"

[Note: At the time, I didn't know the specific location. I received an update soon after.]

Update: Mothman Sighting, Middletown, Ohio.

I received an update to this sighting including another related encounter. This creature (or creatures) may continue to visit in the area:

"Well, both my friend and I live closer to Middletown, OH. There was another encounter I had shortly after I had sent the email and I kept forgetting that I hadn't sent it. I had walked out of my room to wash my face, try and calm myself down, etc. and my brother's room is directly across the hall from mine. I looked straight ahead and it was looking right through the window of his room (that's the picture I had sent). I stared at it for a while, feeling kind of cold and then feeling really scared and I finally pulled my eyes away and went about my business. When I came out of my bathroom, I didn't look in the direction of his room. My friend reported that what she saw had more oblique-shaped eyes and looked kind of 'angry' (I wasn't too sure about that hypothesis), while mine had large, round eyes and seemed kind of curious or something.

Sorry I didn't include that in the original message; like I said, this happened after I sent the email and I keep assuming I had included it when I hadn't. Other than the weird sightings, there wasn't any strange activity I can recall."

Mothman Comes Home.

I received the following email from a woman in Ohio who had concerns in reference to a sighting her and a girlfriend had six months prior to the report. She stated that she substituted their names for anonymity. 'Megan' affirms that all other details, location, date and description of the incident are factual:

"Sir, my name is Megan. I am forwarding a summary of an experience that I and a friend had in August 2010. My friend and associate Kyra and I traveled from Columbus, Ohio to Ravenswood, West Virginia on business. While we were there, I wanted to make a side trip to Gallipolis, Ohio in order to visit relatives I had not seen for quite a while.

After our meeting and presentation, we drove onto Ohio Rt. 7 and traveled south along the Ohio River towards Gallipolis. We had a nice, though brief, visit with my relatives. Around 6PM, we left their home and drove a few miles north on Rt. 7 to check-in to a hotel near the local airport.

Around 7:30PM, we decided to get dinner and found a quiet restaurant so we could eat and work. After we finished, Kyra needed to go to the store and pick up a few items that she forgot to pack. We headed to a Wal-Mart that was nearby the restaurant.

After we finished shopping, we were walking to the car when I noticed a woman running through the parking lot. When she reached her car, she looked back in the direction of the store then hurriedly got into the car. I quickly looked in the same direction and saw what looked like a large bird flying above the roof of the store. It was difficult to see but when it swooped downward the parking lot lights would shine off of it. It looked like it was either oily or had shiny leather-like skin. Whatever it was, it had a wide wing span. I would guess it reached 8-10 foot across. It circled above the store for about a minute then just disappeared.

We were both somewhat shocked at what we witnessed but figured that it was just a huge bird. Since it was dark, I figured we had misjudged what it really was.

We drove back to the hotel and decided to call it a night so we could get an early start on the drive home in the morning. I got ready for bed but thought I'd watch some television first. By this time it was around 10PM or so.

I must have dozed off fairly quickly because the next thing I remember is frantic knocking on my door. I stumbled out of bed and checked who it was. It was Kyra and she was obviously upset. She rushed into my room and said "it's here!" "What are you talking about?" A little bit perturbed that she woke me up. She said that she was laying on the bed reading when she heard something in the hallway. She got out of bed, walked to the door and listened to what she thought was 'scratching' sounds. After a few minutes the sounds stopped, so she went back to bed. Not long after she lay down she heard more scratching sounds but, from outside her window. Again she got up and peeked through the curtains. This time, something looked back at her.

Our rooms were on the second floor in the back section of the hotel and both looked out onto a small parking lot and a large field beyond that. She could see, what she described as, a 'bald ugly man with wings' who was looking directly at her with 'large bulging eyes that lit up bright red.' It was there for only a few seconds. It then spread its wings while running at the same time towards the end of the parking lot and lifted off the ground like a bird.

"You're kidding, right?" I muttered to her. "Meg, I swear to God - that thing is out there and it knows we saw it!" I knew the only way I was going to get some sleep was to allow Kyra to stay in my room. The next morning we woke early, checked out and drove back to Columbus.

Kyra didn't mention the incident from the previous night during the ride. In fact, she has still never said anything else about it. We continue to be good friends and have a very good working relationship.

But I got curious. I had never heard about the Mothman or any of the tales associated with it. I grew up in Texas and had only lived in Ohio for a few years. I moved into my Mom's house after she had passed away. Her relatives lived throughout Ohio but I had never been told any of the stories.

This is the reason I am writing to you. We were near Point Pleasant, WV when we had this encounter. Do you think that it is possible that this was a Mothman? I read some of your posts recently and I'm starting to believe that Kyra actually saw something supernatural.

In light of the prophecies of danger that this thing is supposed to warn people about, Kyra has had some bad luck and tragedy since that day.

Her husband suddenly left her, she had a fire in her house and she severely injured her leg in a fall. Could this be connected?

I personally don't believe in predictions, either good or bad. But I will admit that these have been strange times since we witnessed 'whatever.'"

[Note: I responded to Megan's concerns with a lot more uncertainty, we really don't have many answers for the Mothman. Is it natural, supernatural or non-terrestrial. Some people think that it may be an escaped experiment performed by the government. What would you tell 'Megan?']

Alaskan Mothman: Dark Harbinger.

I received this email from a young man in Alaska (unedited):

"My first encounter with this thing most people call the Mothman was when I was nine years old and I remember it clearly like it was yesterday. I was walking back from my uncle's place. I was walking on the sidewalk and I saw this man standing on top of my father's house close to the edge facing west. He was all black he looked like a man. He stood about 7 or 8 feet tall. I shouted out at him but he acted like he didn't hear me. I said "hey you, who are you?" I kept trying to get his attention, it was like I wasn't there. But when I said "hey, you're standing on my house, who are you?" he looked at me for a few seconds.

His face seemed like a normal persons face until it slowly opened its eyelids and I saw a red glow, like his eyes were glowing, not a red light but a glow. I froze and just stared at him. He stood there looking at me for 9 or 10 seconds and looked away and jumped really high and far. I'd say he jumped about 40 feet high and 70 to 80 feet away and as soon as he seemed to fall down, very long and large wings came out of his back and flapped twice, just in those two flaps he traveled about 100 feet and flew right over the high school.

Since that day I never spoke to anyone about it because I thought I saw the devil. I freaked out so bad, I looked out for it every day to make sure it wasn't around. That is my first encounter with that thing. Its body was like a man's and his face is like a man's too, but his eyes are what make it so scary and weird. Those wings are very long and large. His whole body was all black, like not skin but blackness was covering him, I can't explain. I'm not the only one in my village that sother villages, even to a point that the thing goes into people's houses while they sleep. That happened to someone I know." -N.H.

59

A few days later, the witness N.H. contacted me again. Before I decided to post further encounters I needed to know more details into these sightings as well as the possibility that similar incidents had been recorded. These specific occurrences where experienced in and around the coastal village of Tununak, Alaska, located on the northeast coast of Nelson Island, about 110 miles northwest of Bethel. The population of the community consists of 96.9% Alaska Native or part Native. Tununak is a traditional Yup'ik Eskimo village, with an active fishing and subsistence lifestyle.

I will be referring to the witness as 'Nate.' There are a few questions that needed to be asked during the research process in particular, why he refers to the being as a 'Mothman':

"I don't know its real name. It's just that all the people here know it as the 'devil,' it comes around and suddenly very bad things start happening. Sometimes it just seems to be watching and nothing happens or very weird things happen. Some people will experience an ability of some sort for a short time and then suddenly they're back to normal. If you ask me I think that the Mothman is not a physical being. I think it's an energy formed from somewhere or someplace that takes character when encountered by an individual. When encountered by a person with a certain belief system the Mothman takes on a form according to the person's point of view of reality. That's one theory of mine to explain its appearance to people. Some people will say it looked like an angel with red eyes. Some will say it looks like a cowboy standing 9 feet tall with glowing red eyes. Others will say it looked like a six feet tall man that can walk through walls. So to tell you my thoughts of the name of the thing I would say maybe its name is 'Leviathan' from the book of Job in the Bible. That would be the closest name I got for it. Why I had so many encounters with it, I have no idea. I do know that there have been encounters in other villages."

The following narratives are Nate's description of his subsequent experiences with this being:

"My second encounter was when I was a teenager. It was a winter night and I was riding on a snowmachine with my cousin. We saw a light on the north hill. We thought it was a snowmachine so we went to go and see who it was. When we got close to the hill the light disappeared. We were able to see every part of the hill, the light just vanished nowhere in sight, so we were gonna go back home. We turned the snowmachine around as cousin said he had to urinate, so I waited for him to finish.

While I was waiting I saw a black object on the ground, darker than all the other things on the ground. It was getting taller like something was coming out of the ground. As soon as it reached 7 feet tall or so it started to come at us fast. I told my cousin to look at the thing. He started to freak out and ran to the snow-machine, started it and looked back at it. He yelled it's getting very close so I looked back. It seemed to be 100 ft. or so away and coming fast. I screamed to my cousin to take off fast. I was so freaked out I closed my eyes. We were going at least 50 miles an hour on the snow-machine. I looked back to see how far we got from it but that thing was getting closer, I estimate at 15 to 20 feet away from us. It was like that thing was not even running and seemed to float over the ground. I couldn't see any eyes on it, no red eyes, just all black. I was screaming to my cousin to go faster but the thing just got closer and closer like speed was nothing to it. When we reached the village the thing stopped and turned around. My cousin just kept going fast on the town road going about 60 miles an hour until we got close to my grandmother's place. He slammed on the brakes as we jumped out of the snow-machine and ran into the house. We told everyone inside about what was chasing us. My grandmother said it was the 'devil' and told us to stop being 'bad kids.'

The third encounter was when I was 22 years old and at home playing on an Ouija board. I was talking with the board and it said it was the 'DEVIL' so I foolish asked it to possess me. It said 'NO.' I asked why, it said 'WRATH' so I stopped asking it questions. Suddenly the room started to get cold even with the furnace running. I wrapped myself with my blanket but I was just getting colder. I also felt the need to look through the window, like something was telling me to. I again felt this urge to look, so I got up, went over to the window and looked outside. I saw a man standing next to the steps of my neighbor's house, just looking at me. I could tell he was staring at me though I thought it was one of my neighbors, so I went outside to talk to him. I called his name but he never replied. The street light was shining on him but I was unable to see his face, like he was covered in a black cloud or some sort of blackness. I kept trying to get him it to recognize me but received no answer from him.

I took out my zippo lighter which I had just filled with lighter fluid and hadn't used it since. I flicked it on and tried to see his face but I still couldn't see it. When I got closer my zippo turned off as if that thing blew at it. I tried to relight it but I was unable to do so. Suddenly I heard a quiet voice saying in my head to 'back away.' So I backed off slowly, not turning my back until I got to the road. When I reached the road I took off running as fast as I could to my place. I looked out the window to see if it was still there and it was still staring at me. I started to look for a flashlight so I could see what or who it was. When I found the flashlight I looked out the window and noticed that it was moving off to the road.

I decided to follow it. When I looked closely it didn't seem to be walking, it was floating away. Dogs would start barking as it passed houses. I was chasing it holding a flashlight hoping I could get a look at his face. I was too slow to get close but fast enough to keep up behind it, like it was going slow to make sure I was behind it but fast enough to stay far ahead of me. It was luring me to him but I kept chasing it. When it started getting closer to the church it slowed down and circled the church, like it didn't want to get close. It continued to move on and I just continued chasing it. When we reached the end of the village I stopped. I felt creeped out, like that thing was trying to get me to go out onto the tundra in the dark. I turned around and quickly walked home.

There are other encounters with this thing that many of the people in the world know as 'Mothman' but here, we know it as the 'Devil' or 'Demon.' He has been around for very long time and has been seen by many people here. He has done a lot of things that creep everyone out, like being at a location where someone dies the very next day and on the very exact spot where he was. When he comes around that means something very bad is going happen.

I don't call him the 'Devil' or 'Demon.' I disagree with that term, I just call him the 'Black Man with Red Eyes' or 'Dark Man' because he's surrounded by a blackness or a black cloud.

There was an encounter where a guy was out hunting and saw it with a couple of his friends. They tried to get its attention but it never responded back. They tried shooting next to it but he never got spooked by the gunshot. There are many other encounters but these are not mine so I can't say exactly what happened, I just hear the stories."

Despite the influence of the Christian missionaries, Yup'ik shamans (angalkuq) possess powers that are beyond physical powers. Their achievements are considered impossible for any human being to accomplish. Shamans define a customary role in Yup'ik life, and while Christian religions have interceded in Yup'ik traditions, some say that shamans still play an important role. A long time ago, Yup'ik forefathers encountered supernatural beings and some have become stories that were passed down from one generation to the next. Encounters of supernatural beings are considered true and can happen to anyone and anybody.

The legends and folklore of the Yup'ik people do include several good and evil spirits but nothing similar to the descriptions given by Nate. The closest traditional entity would be of a dark shaman who makes life more difficult for the people around them. There is nothing that would represent a harbinger of death.

During my research I was impressed by Yup'ik customs, especially those that involved gossip, lies and their respect for spirituality. The community, even in current times, deeply frowns upon malice towards others and the spread of distorted accounts. Because of these traditions and fear of ridicule, there is little to wonder as to why these stories have not reached the mainstream.

Mothman Sighting, Mertztown, PA.

Mertztown is in Longswamp Township in eastern Berks County, Pennsylvania. The witness wrote me after reading one of my previous reports (unedited):

"Good morning, as I sit reading this article, it amazes me that no one caught one of these things yet. I understand that if something with a 25-30ft wingspan flies past you, you're not going to grab your camera as a first instinct.

My son and I saw this monster thing last summer in Mertztown, PA. We were parked on the side of the road in a heavily wooded area when this thing casually glided up the road. It looked big enough to carry a full grown man away with no effort. When the wing flew over the hood of my car, we instantly ducked down. This thing had a round human sized head with no beak (hence the term man-bird), and huge bat-like wings. Now I would never tell this story if it wasn't for my 16-yr-old son sitting in the backseat who also witnessed it on that summer day. I'm a pretty capable guy, not too many things can shake me, but this thing scared the hell out of me. Here is what I saw:

The body was 5-6ft in length easy, wing span was 25-30ft easy, no feathers, bat like skin, jet black, and a 4-5ft skinny (rat or dragon) like tail that stuck straight out. This thing didn't fly like a bird, it glided about 10ft off the ground at a VERY slow speed. After 50-75ft of gliding, it took one huge flap of the wings, never changing elevation, and glided up the road till it disappeared into the woods. I'm convinced this thing lives underground, probably near some sort of hot spring because it has no feathers.

Well that's my story. Feel free to reply with any questions, that 45 second event will forever be etched into memory. I say we find it and catch it, I would love to see it again up close."

Encounter, New Miami, Ohio.

New Miami is in central Butler County in the southwestern part of Ohio. The witness wrote me after searching the internet for answers (unedited):

"On Monday May 9th, 2011 around 5:45am, I was on my way to work headed north bound in to the village of New Miami on Seven Mile Avenue. I left the traffic light at the southern-most edge of town in to a dark stretch of road when a large flying creature swooped in over my car and snatched up a small animal in the road ahead of me at the edge of my head lights. As a construction worker, I feel I can judge the size of objects fairly well. This creature had a wing span of at least 12 feet and was jet black with a human figure. It completely blocked the view out of my windshield and then some and moved at a very high rate of speed. I was traveling between 35-40MPH. It had to have been traveling at around 70-80MPH. Like I stated before is swooped down grabbed the animal and was gone over the trees very quickly. I've researched large predator birds and raptors indigenous to Ohio and there are none that fit the description of what I saw. If you have any other questions about my experience please feel free to email me back." -T.

The North Georgia Mothman.

In December 2011 I received an email from a woman (who I will refer to as 'EW') from north Georgia who thought she had encountered a Mothman. After many months of correspondence, the witness has agreed to allow me to post the event but only under strict circumstances. She has reviewed this post and has agreed to the following content being published:

"Hello, I am hoping you can shed some light on an incident I had a few years ago. I was twenty-five at the time and was driving to my friend CW's house. It was quiet at 11:30 pm as I drove south on an old country road off of (redacted) highway near (redacted) in north Georgia. Very few people pass this way because it leads to nothing but a small group of houses. I turned on the radio but nothing came on. I figured it was a blown fuse but then I started to hear weird scratching sounds coming through the speakers. It sounded like a distant voice but I couldn't understand what it was saying.
Suddenly, something flew in front of the car and hit the windshield with enough size and force that it totally mangled the grill and hood. I immediately stopped the car. I heard what sounded like wings flapping on the roof, but then something rolled down the back window onto the

trunk then eventually on to the road. I thought I killed whatever it was. A woman in a truck had pulled up from behind and said she saw the thing hit the road. She said that its eyes were glaring bright red. As we looked more closely at this thing it resembled a man with large bat-like wings. The woman walked back to her truck and pulled a shotgun from the back and pointed it at this bat-like creature.

It was starting to move and we backed off. It slowly stood up on two large raptor-like claws, turned and stared directly at us with those terrible bright red eyes. The woman pumped the shotgun. It slowly levitated off the ground with wings spread until it was about 10 foot up then instantly, it let out a deafening screech as it just disappeared with a loud 'swoosh.' The woman (who I found out later was CW's aunt) and I just looked at each other.

This thing had the body of a well-built man. It had no feathers but charcoal gray skin like that of a bat with some hair on the shoulders and around the eyes and legs. When it spread its wings, it had the span of 12 foot or more. I estimate it was about 8 foot tall. It had no head however, just the eyes embedded on the shoulders that had brows. I didn't notice a mouth or nose. There is no way I was going to report this and CW's aunt totally agreed. We both drove off to CW's house. I was so shook up I stayed the night.

The next morning, I went outside to inspect the car. There was a huge crack in the windshield and the grill was mangled beyond repair. The hood also had a deep 25 inch dent. I started to walk back to the house when I noticed something lying in the grass beside the garage. It was CW's Golden Retriever lying dead from massive lacerations up and down its back. I just knew that thing did it.

That was three years ago and I constantly dream of this creature. I was told by a friend that I had encountered a Mothman. It looked more like a Batman to be honest. I decided to look up a few of the sightings by others and saw your name and blog. Many of the images on Google were very similar to what I saw. I wrote to someone else about a year ago but they never got back to me. I have included two of the images I think look the most like the creature I hit with my car that night. Could you contact me at this email? Thank you for your time. -*EW*

[Note: I contacted EW and tried to answer her questions. I have no doubt she witnessed a winged humanoid and most likely a Mothman. She agreed to let me post the incident provided I leave out several of the more personal points from the original email. I will say that EW has experienced many of the same anomalous events claimed by a few of the original Point Pleasant, WV witnesses, including some I discovered myself through research and witness interviews.']

Communion with the Mothman.

I received this account from a colleague who had previously shared her paranormal experiences with me. The following remarkable narrative may very well add credence to the Mothman phenomena and, frankly, I have no reason not to believe the story. I have not edited the original text except for a few minor errors. I realize that the allegory is a bit hard to follow at certain spots, but I wanted to save the integrity of the writer's thoughts and emotion. This narrative was originally posted a few years ago and resulted in quite a bit of feedback:

In 1967, two weeks before the collapse of the Silver Bridge, a phone call came to our house south of Lancaster, Ohio. It was from dad's friends in southwestern W.Va. Someone else in our house answered the phone and dad was busy watching the evening news so he yelled to whoever answered it to ask them what they wanted. The answer was that they had some trouble over in W.Va. and needed dad to come down. He asked what the trouble was and the person on the other end said it was a big bird. Well, we'd just seen a piece on this on the news and the anchor who reported it laughed about it. Dad laughed and said that was a good one and to tell the person this and then hang up.

A short time after the phone rang again. This was when long distance cost an arm and a leg so dad asked what was going on and again it was that they had this big bird that had done a lot of damage and they needed help to hunt it down. He took the phone call then and we all heard him saying, "All of my guns and all of my ammunition?? What the heck is going on down there?" There were a couple of okays and then I heard him ask why this man's daughter needed to talk to me. It was explained to me that this youngest girl had what they thought was an imaginary friend but asking to talk with me was a good sign that she was coming out of this mentally and emotionally and I was to play along. It was supposed to be for her own good. I was nine years old and she was maybe a few months behind me. I got on the phone and she asked if this was (my name) and I said yes. I asked what her name was and she said what it was. I'd met her once before and she was very introverted and really didn't mix with us. She showed us rocks and bugs but didn't really get involved in getting to know us. That's why I was shocked that this girl asked for me by name. I told her she had a good memory and she said it wasn't her memory that she got my name from! I thought, OK, she's a bit touched as they say, LOL.

66

I asked where she got my name in order to ask for me and she said it was her friend who was a man, but wasn't a man. I said, "Okay, who is this friend and what does he want with me?" She began to relate that in the course of talking one day he told her my name and said he wanted her to contact me and ask me to come down there to talk to him. I said I'd have to talk to my parents first. I got off the phone and dad wanted to know what was up with this girl. I said there was no way she knew my name. He asked where she got it then. I told him and he got a little alarmed and called their house to ask some questions about this man that 'wasn't a man' and who he might be. They assured him that it wasn't anyone near them as they were out on a quiet country road with only a few neighbors. She said this friend of hers wasn't one of them. They'd checked the woods where she said she'd met with him and never found any footprints or signs that anyone had been there with her. So, because this was urgent we packed up quick and headed down there from central Ohio.

We waited in line to cross the Silver Bridge across from Point Pleasant. A cross member on the top of this bridge on our side of the river was swinging back and forth as it was not attached on one end. The bridge clanged and made all sorts of racket when a car was crossing it. I was told to sit back and rest my eyes because the sunlight was very bright that day and I was getting hot. I felt my eyes get heavy, like I was slipping right into a comfortable rest. The next thing I knew I heard screaming and found myself horizontal above my brothers clawing at the window screaming to be let out that the bridge was going to go into the river. Dad got me calmed down and asked when this was going to happen. I had to rest, I was exhausted. So, I sat back slipped once again and again, found myself across my brothers with my siblings holding my legs and ankles to keep me from going out the window. I realized I was screaming again and clawing at the window. I asked what was going on and they all said I'd been OK and then suddenly lunged for the window to claw my way out while screaming hard. Mom said to beat me for it and so did my siblings. Dad on the other hand told them to hush while he walked me through what I was seeing when I woke up doing this.

I was in a vehicle and it was falling off that bridge into the river below and I saw every inch of the fall to the water and below the water even. I was horrified when it was slow enough for me to see all of this clearly. Dad asked if we'd get across OK that day and when we were supposed to go back home. I searched my mind and saw it was OK to cross. He had me tell him what would cause the bridge to fall and then show it to him on the other side once we got there. When he saw what I'd seen in my mind on the Ohio side before we got to the W.Va. side he was utterly horrified.

Structurally that bridge should not have been in use at all. I won't go into that part but to say that I got it absolutely right on each and every count. He was quiet all the way there except occasionally he would ask me when this would happen. I remember looking in my mind and telling him it would happen in about two weeks. Two weeks to the day we were sitting watching the TV when a news alert came across to say it had fallen into the river. Mom got a calendar right away and checked it to make sure how long it had been. She cried a bit and then asked me to come over to her. She thanked me for saving all their lives. I'd forgotten all about what happened two weeks prior because it was traumatic not just for my visions but for what happened at the people's house!

I hope this helps others, Lon, but I can't have identifying information come back to me about this for certain reasons. I will continue. We drove a long time before arriving and dad went in to talk to these people as we set up our tent to sleep outside. The man came out and said to put it away because we wouldn't want to be sleeping out there with the troubles they had down there. It didn't make sense to any of us how a big bird could be scaring these people that bad but they were scared badly. While the adults got the low down we kids went up into the woods to take care of the imaginary friend thing. The older kids checked everything out to make sure there was no one and nothing to harm us when they left. We were not far into the woods and it was not all that thick with growth. The driveway was pretty wide and it was a sunny day. They all left and I put my younger brother with her brother about 15 ft. from us at the edge of the woods. We all grew up in the woods so there was nothing any of us didn't know how to deal with if confronted with it. We were well practiced. I just wanted to get this over with but the girl was being timid. She said I'd think she was nuts. I laughed and said that sometimes people don't understand but they need to give it time to sink in. I gained her confidence and so she opened up.

She said "he" would scare me if I saw him straight on. I said there wasn't much that scared me anymore with three brothers that challenged my life at every turn. She looked worried and said he was special and didn't look like us. Well, I thought he was disfigured or something but no that wasn't it either. I said that sooner or later if I was to talk to this man I'd have to see him in order to understand what he wanted to tell me. I was thinking that maybe there was some wildlife around there that she wasn't familiar with that she couldn't see clearly so it had scared her. No, she said that wasn't it either. She said I had to promise not to look unless he said it was OK. I said I didn't want to be close to him then if I needed to take off in a hurry. She said I couldn't do that because it would upset him. I let out a "Ha!" And she just gave me a look and said this was very important to her because he'd been very nice to her and been a good

68

friend when she had no others. Okay, so I appeased her a bit and said I'd play along and be extra nice so I could get this over with. She kept saying not to be alarmed and said she had been the first time she saw him. She said he was very big. I was thinking she must have lost it bad.

I saw movement and there was something looking like a very tall spindly marionette up next to these skinny tall trees. I asked her how she and her siblings had accomplished that. I was laughing but she was looking at me like she had no idea what I was talking about. Then it walked out from the trees without any visible support! I was like okay, there's got to be a sensible explanation to this so I asked if I could move forward after a while to get a better look. I told her I could take this. Well, she asked him and said he said it was OK. Before that though he wanted to talk to my mind, she said. I thought, oh my God, she's really in La La Land, poor girl, stuck in the sticks of W.Va. and she's lost it! Well that thing moved again as if shifting from side to side in a standing position. That was human like. I begin to hear this man's voice in my mind and it's conversing with me. It's all like 'happy to talk to me finally' and 'so excited by my coming to see him.' I thought I'd caught this girl's insanity and hit myself at the side of my head to shake this voice out of my head. She asked what was wrong. I told her! She said that was normal. I had news for her but not yet! I had been ordered to see what this was about. This voice seems to be rifling through all my memories like wildfire and then downloading high quality video, like being there in my mind about that bridge falling and other things in the future. I thought my mind was playing tricks on me so I tried to maintain my balance mentally by reminding myself that I was just playing along and this would all play out to be an elaborate hoax.

I inched closer and closer to the edge of this driveway and then a drop off where the bulldozer had shoved the dirt for it. Movement caught my eyes and I looked down to see these big orange bird feet! I thought, "Oh my God what is that doing in the woods!" I took a very slow, very meticulous look up the legs attached to these feet and they looked stork-like. The feet shifted by one picking up and then the other doing it. It was human like in movement but also bird like. I let my eyes go very slowly up the legs, to the body, and then the chest. Also because I could count the ribs! There appeared to be scant feathers on its skin which was greyish. It was a mix of this bright green color and greyish brown. The more I looked the worse it got but I gritted my teeth and kept my thinking to a minimum. I looked at these wings folded behind its back but yet out a bit to the sides. I could see through them a bit but they looked leathery and stretchy. I looked at the shoulders which in truth were topped with sharp bumps which I realized were from the wings being folded behind its body. I inadvertently got a good look at its head and a wave of revulsion hit me and I said I was going to just back up slowly to get a better look from a distance. I think it picked up that I was scared of it. I heard it in my mind again and it was upset that I was scared of it. I explained with my mind, crazy as that sounds, just thinking I'd seen some people who were disfigured in my time and this was scary too. I'd just have to get used to it. I did want to get out of there with my life unscathed. This was nuts. This thing wanted to chat with me and I wanted to go to the bathroom really bad. I told the girl this and she said we'd have to go to the house. He told her, and I heard it too, that he knew I was scared and he was very upset. Then, he got into a part of my mind that showed what I went through at home and somewhere else, a big building in a big city that I didn't remember except in bits. He was livid at me seeing the entire breadth of whatever that was about. I told them both out loud that this wasn't right for this girl or myself to be talking to him.

He said his kind didn't want any of them mixing with us because it was dangerous for them. He'd shown me where they were from, and it wasn't this planet. I was feeling dizzy and my brother saw me stagger a bit. I said I had to go and this girl had to help me down to the house, so we were going to leave now and she and I were about to be in big trouble because I wasn't allowed to keep such a secret. I got out of the woods OK and got up against their garage and wet my pants. Then I felt like I was losing control of my body and was shaking all over. My brother went and got dad. I told him to stay close to the garage because it was out there somewhere and it was huge. He thought I was nuts but I told him sternly that this man that wasn't a man but was a huge creature with wings and big orange feet. He laughed and I said "I wasn't laughing and we had to get into the house."

We all got into the house and the girl was livid with me for saying I wasn't supposed to tell and now he was angry with her. My head hurt really badly. The adults got their guns out. Phone calls were made and in short order men with guns in pickups and cars came flying into their driveway. Dad wouldn't allow me to tell mom or that woman what I'd seen no one. I wanted to cry but felt stunned, shocked, it was very hard. They got me cleaned up and we all sat trying to be quiet. We tried to listen to what was going on.

That was an awful experience. The men went into the woods leaving the women with guns. They soon came back as it was almost dark. We began to see these huge stick looking figures darting past the picture window out front and then the back windows, and the kitchen door and windows. There was more than one of them. All the guns got loaded and we were put into the middle of the house. There was clawing at the roof, siding and windows. This went on for hours and I finally just went to sleep. I was hot and probably in shock so I just went to sleep.

Everything eventually went quiet and it stayed that way for hours. I woke up needing to go to the bathroom. There was a window so someone had to stand there with a gun as I went. Something came to the window and began to claw at it. By then I didn't know what this was or why it was happening. I was given a magazine and put my whole mind on it and read. When I did this all stopped outside. I got tired and quit doing that while wondering what was going on and it began all over again. We could all hear the tin being torn off the roof. I went back to sleep and everything was quiet the rest of what was left of the night.

The next day we packed up and started home. Dad asked before we got to the bridge if we'd be OK crossing it. I looked in my mind and saw it was OK. They wanted to know this over and over again. I was sure. On the Ohio side of the river my brothers and sisters began to talk about what was going on. Something big swooped down at the car and began to claw at it. This happened off and on all the way home. We could hear this thing holding on to the top of the car!! Once home I was sent to my room and told to go to sleep. Well, I didn't. I was listening to what they were saying downstairs. One of my brothers ran downstairs and said there was noise on the roof. Dad told them to go outside and look to see what it was. My brother returned pale looking and said it was a huge bird like thing with glowing red eyes. Dad said that wasn't funny. My brother said he knew it wasn't but this was true. Dad went out and sure enough he came back to say yes it was true. They were all upset and I was up under the roof that was being torn off. My family was watching shingles coming through the air and landing on the ground out back and front. They got the guns out and I was told to lay down and go to sleep. It was OK for a while but then it started again.

My brother came to me and said to look out my window. He told me to look at these little red glowing lights outside. They were eyes. I could see huge spindly wings out there walking around on the ground. It was like they were on their elbows. It was really creepy. Dad took a gun out and then I heard him yell to me saying they were going to hurt him if I didn't say he never hurt me. I said I wasn't allowed to tell lies and he asked me nicely to be nice for him. So, I did. I told them I was OK and I was with my siblings who were older and took care of me. He was scared and we could see several of them out there near him. We saw him back slowly into the door.

I felt they were in my mind asking what I wanted most in life. I remember thinking I just wanted to run around and have fun like other kids did. I went to sleep and it was quiet until about 2 am. I woke up to the sound of my older brother's voice asking what we were doing outside with these things and what were they. How did I get outside? My younger brother was behind me and we were running through what I thought was a tunnel on the lawn. I woke up more and saw it was these things lined up with their wings arched over like a tunnel and we'd been running through them! I was horrified and our older brother saw this. He said dad had sent him out and dad was hanging out the window telling us quietly that it was OK, we weren't in trouble but we should come in because it's really late. I looked at my brothers and asked what was wrong with dad. The older brother said dad was really scared to come outside because those things wanted to hurt him. I asked how he could tell! He laughed a little and said he'd never seen him like this before and said he'd woke him up and "asked" him to go out and get us back in the house. We both dropped our jaws and said, "He asked you?"

We went inside and went right to bed before we got beat for it. We never did and the next day it was like no one wanted to talk about it. My younger brother kept asking what those things were and wasn't it funny that dad was so scared of them. My head hurt. I was diagnosed with traumatic childhood amnesia in 1983 but I have a photographic memory. Okay, so I had no memory of these things until some years later. It was difficult to wrap my head around all of this, still is. Earlier this year, end of Feb. 2011 I started to again hear the voice of this thing in my mind. It showed me ripples in a pond. I didn't know what that was supposed to be for and I was busy working so I pushed it out of my mind. My mind was being pulled to Middletown, Ohio on the map. I thought OK, what's this about, spit it out, I'm pretty busy these days. No explanation.

This continued and still is happening even now. I was looking at other things about archaeology and up comes information about the thunderbird, dragons, snakes, and how it applies to Native American culture. I'm Shawnee and a direct descendant of Tecumseh. I've still got this unknown 'man' in my mind and he seems to want to chat but I'm thinking these things eat people and people have been known to disappear after seeing these things. I'm thinking I was lucky and blessed to be alive after seeing it that close twice! So, Lon, if you would, say a prayer for me. I'm still very busy with work, photography for home inspections and craft work I have at home. Still from time to time this voice is in my mind. This thing wants to be friends with me but there seems to be something important he wants to convey to me.

I just keep shoving it out of my head. I'm not so sure this thing isn't evil. I mean it did kill a big dog over in W.Va. in 1967. It or they tore it into tiny bits and there wasn't much left of it. If you'd like to turn this into a report I'm sure it would take a lot of work to take out anything that would ID me in any way. I want people to be helped by knowing that these things are real. I can't explain what they are about but I know they are real. Thanks. -DR

Messenger, Harbinger or Omen?

I received an email in response to several of the Mothman related posts made on 'Phantoms and Monsters.' I attempted to keep the content as original as possible:

"Hello sir, a friend referred me to your articles about strange occurrences in West Virginia. The Mothman encounters stirred memories of an incident that took place when I was a girl.

The strange incident took place near Powellton, WV in December 1934, I was 8 years old. At the time, my father worked for Elkhorn-Piney Coal. He and the other miners from our area would take a train to the mine each day.

The day before Christmas Eve my father mentioned an unusual sighting he and the others on the train had while traveling back home that evening. As they looked out towards the east they noticed a very large bird flying above the trees. My father was a very conservative man and didn't believe in any nonsense but this large bird really caught his attention. He described it as a freakish sized owl very dark in color. It also seemed to look at the train as it flew over the trees. Nobody on the train could figure out what it was. The mere fact that my father even mentioned it suggested that it must have been an extraordinary sight.

My father was scheduled off from work for 3 days during the Christmas holiday. On December 27th, he was getting ready for work but said he felt poorly. My mother was concerned because he had a high fever and awful chills. She insisted he stay home and telephoned the doctor. My father was reluctant on staying home and put up a good argument but my mother was not going to back down. She put him to bed and waited for the doctor.

Well, we waited for hours until the telephone rang. The operator told my mother that the doctor was at McDunn, there had been a horrible train explosion. She couldn't talk but said that the doctor's wife asked her to contact us. My mother was pale when she told my father what had happened. I remember they both started praying and crying. For years both of them thought the large bird was an angel sent by God as a warning and that my father's life was saved for a reason.

My father never went back to the mine. It turned out that he had contracted polio though he was very lucky since he survived it with only a slight limp. We soon moved away to a small town in Kentucky where my father found the calling and become a Pentecostal preacher. He told his story of survival to anyone who would listen until the day he died. Thank you sir, Emma

[Note: the disaster that Emma was referring to was the 'Locomotive Boiler Explosion at McDunn.' On December 27, 1934, a boiler in a locomotive hauling mine workers at McDunn in Fayette County, WV exploded, resulting in the death of eighteen miners.]

Mothman Sighting near Huntington, WV.

I received this information from Mike P., a colleague in Chesapeake, Ohio. I was given the witness contact email at the time. I received a response today. The following is the original email:

"Hello, a friend suggested I write to you about something that happened to me several weeks ago. I am divorced and have 2 boys, 15 and 12 years old. Both of my sons were with me at the time of the incident. We live in Huntington, West Virginia, moved here in 2009 from Milwaukee, WI because of my job.

On March 2nd, we were travelling south on Rt. 2 (Ohio River Rd.) just outside of Huntington near Cox Landing Rd. It was around 8:30 PM, we were on our way back home after visiting a co-worker. About a mile past the intersection I noticed something flying from behind a house on the right side. It was hard to make out at first but as it came towards the road it looked like a huge butterfly. Even though it was dark the light from the side of the house illuminated it enough that I could make out a shape. I sped up to avoid coming in contact with this thing but as I did it circled around and flew just ahead of us on our right side. The wings were enormous and broad like that of a butterfly. It was strange because I never saw it flap the wings, almost like it was gliding. My boys were now aware of it and were terrified. I didn't want to stop the car so I decided to speed up some more. After about 20 seconds it suddenly shot up into the air and disappeared.

One thing I want to mention is that we were under severe storm and flash flood warnings that evening. There were some high wind gusts and hail. There had been several tornadoes southwest of us in Kentucky.

When we got home we talked about it, my oldest boy said it looked like a person dressed in a black shiny suit. He didn't see legs or feet but said the body shape looked like a tall thin man. My youngest boy said he didn't get a very good look but felt like something bad was going to happen. My description is very similar to my oldest son's, but the wings were massive and broad. I'd say the wings may have been over twice the size of the body. The entire thing was dark colored but there was a faint orange glow from the head area, I never noticed a face or other features.

Last week I was talking to a friend and told her about the incident. She found your name and contact information and forwarded it to me. She mentioned something about Mothman sightings in this area and I read some of the stories. I'm not sure if this is the same thing but it does fit the description. There were a few drawings on Google, some are close to what I saw but don't generally match the wing size.

If you have questions please use my email. I'm more curious of what I saw and anything else you can offer. I don't want to believe the Mothman stories but maybe you have an explanation. Thank you for your time" -N.R.

[Note: I received a response from N.R. the next morning. Her estimation to the size of this being is a thin 5' body and a wing span of 12-15'. Also that it was black and shiny like 'polished black leather'. N.R. believes that her top speed was around 60 MPH and that it easily kept in front of her. She agreed to me publishing the encounter though she doesn't want any personal information disclosed. She was very curious as to what they witnessed. BTW, the location of this sighting is approximately 30 miles south of Point Pleasant, WV.]

Chapter 5

Large Flying Creature, Medina River, Texas.

I received this email from a man who lives west of San Antonio, Texas near Medina Lake. He states he witnessed a large flying creature on the evening of August 11, 2009. He requested that his full name be withheld at the present time. (Note: edited for typos only)

"Dear Sir. I witnessed a large flying creature this evening that I cannot identify. I found your site during a search. I'm apprehensive of mentioning it to any friends or family until I can get a grip on what this was.

I live west of San Antonio, TX near Medina Lake. Today, I was on a random outing to the area near the Diversion Lake dam. At about 7:30 pm, I was on my way back up the trail when I suddenly heard a loud awful scream coming from below the dam downstream. It sounded like an owl but lasted longer and was much louder. I stopped walking and watched downstream to see if I could catch a look at what caused the sound.

I then noticed a large flock of birds flush out of the trees near the riverbank. Then suddenly this giant flying creature swooped down into the river valley and just as quickly flew back up into the rocks. I continued to watch but did not hear or see it again. I call it a creature because it looked nothing like a bird. I was about 50 yards from it and would say conservatively that its wing span was 15 ft. or so! It was dark colored and had a very long beak and a strange long thin tail. This sounds crazy, but it actually resembled one of those flying dinosaurs though the head was not as large and it looked like it had feathers.

I got back home and looked on the internet for examples of bird species but found nothing close. I'm not originally from this area and have never heard of anything like this. That is why I'm contacting you. Do you have an idea what it was? I see you have a website, maybe someone who reads your site could help identify it." -*JJ*

[Note: there are many 'Thunderbird' legends in the area and there have been a few related sightings in and around San Antonio and further south.]

Encounter with a Shape Shifter.

"I was with a group of people on Saturday, August 8th in Central Arkansas (out in the country) right before dusk. This area has one lane bridges with gravel roads and no road name signs. Many years ago this had been an Amish community. One of the people I was with had lived there when she was a child. We had returned to the area to go ghost hunting at a cemetery near her old home. None of us are drinkers or drug users and are all middle aged. We belong to a local ghost hunter's club, but this night, we were on our own.

We arrived well before dusk to make sure we had a good feel for our surroundings. I stepped out of the car and walked maybe 6 feet when I heard the sound of something quickly approaching me. It sounded like wings flapping, but not the same. Hard to describe really. It was on a much larger scale than I had heard before. I quickly turned around and saw this thing headed right for me. I was so scared I could not image what I was seeing. I screamed and hit the ground. It flew over my head and landed on the tree limb near me. I looked up and saw it looking down at me, I turned as my friends called my name and was running to me. When I looked back, I couldn't see it. My friends witnessed it as it flew towards me though they didn't see it in the tree.

It didn't look the same in the tree that it had looked while flying toward me. In the tree, it looked more like a large worm or snake but much, much larger. It looked as if it had wrapped it's self around the tree limb. A bird can't do that. I did look to see if there were any other reports like this area, but did not find any documented. I am now afraid to go outside before dusk in fear of seeing another one. I have never been scared ghost hunting. This thing was the most amazing, scariest thing, I have ever seen in my life. I pray I never see it again. Do you have any idea what this thing was? A shape shifter or possibly a Thunderbird? Maybe a demon? I have no idea."

'Monster' Sighting, Raystown Lake, PA.

I received the following email in reference to an unusual sighting on 8/29/2009. Full name and other identification was held back by request:

"I was referred to you by a friend. Can you advise or direct me to someone who can explain what I witnessed?

On August 29, 2009, I was fishing from a boat with my son on Raystown Lake, Pa. It was around 6:45 pm and we were making our way back to the landing. We were near the Snydertown portion of the lake where there is a point of land.

As we were heading south, I looked toward the west shore after my son started to point at something. I really have NO idea what this thing was but it looked like a large, thick black snake with a huge head that bobbed in and out of the water. I moved a little bit closer but my son was getting scared, so I cut the motor and looked through my binoculars. The body was moving in coils or humps up and down in the water. The creature had no fins like a fish and the head was diamond shaped. The weirdest feature was that the eyes (which were dark, somewhat small and slanted) were not set on the side of the head, but placed forward. I got an excellent look through the binoculars (I'd say it was about 50 yards from us) when it rose up, its head moved side to side. It made no sound. I'd say it was at least 20 feet long.

I have lived in Altoona, Pa for only a few years and this is only the second time I have fished this lake. I'm from Wisconsin and have fished many large lakes and rivers but I have never seen anything this big.

We watched for about 2-3 minutes until it slipped under the surface. My son's description was very similar to mine but he said he noticed lighter colored 'whiskers' or rays on the chin and face while looking through the binoculars. I had tried to take a photo with my cell phone but it just blended in with the water and was not discernible.

My son found an image on the internet that closely resembled what we witnessed. This is nuts! My friends think we saw a large fish or mammal, but there is no way it's either. Please give me some guidance or resources to help identify this. I am skeptical of monsters, ghosts, ufo's, etc. and don't buy into much of what people describe on TV. But, now that I have seen something that I can't explain, let's say I'm confused and frustrated. Thanks, -*Bill*"

[Note: I used to fish this very lake years ago (excellent striped bass fishing!). I knew that there were some reports of a 'monster' sighted there a while back but have not heard anything lately. Anyway, Raystown Lake is a very deep water man-made lake located in Huntingdon County, Pa., east of Altoona, Pa. and south of State College, Pa. I emailed back to the witness 'Bill.' He seems to be very sincere about this sighting. He stated that he reported it to another paranormal site but didn't get a response.]

Update: I had a few questions for 'Bill' so I sent him an email asking him to attach the photos he took with his cellphone. I wanted to see for myself what he meant by 'but it just blended in with the water and was not discernible.' He forwarded two photos which I examined. Since he and his son were on the same level as the creature there was a dark background of the trees as well as some glare coming off the water. I tried to enhance the photos, but there was just nothing with any definition though I could make out some disturbance on the surface of the water. There wasn't much more information that he could offer, but I certainly believe he and his son witnessed something unusual.

I found a video and a few images from 2006. This creature is referred to as 'Raystown Ray.' Honestly, I never gave these sightings much consideration but may look into this further now that a supposed witness has come forward to me.

Flying Cryptid in West Virginia.

"I saw something very similar to what was described in one of your articles. My sighting occurred in a rural area of Henderson, West Virginia, approximately 20 years ago (1989). I had been visiting a friend with my daughter and was on my way home in the afternoon. The day was partly sunny with clouds in the sky, but not rainy or misty. We were traveling down an incline in the car and we saw something strange go across the road (from the left side to the right side of the road). I'm not good with distances but it was probably no more than fifty feet from us. The thing described in the article was much smaller than what my daughter and I saw. I watched it disappear and asked my daughter if she had seen anything, and she confirmed that she had seen it also.

What we observed was approximately horse or cow sized and it had a white, translucent appearance, without identifiable head, tail, or appendages. It was just a big oval shaped airy "blob" that you could see through! This thing was like watching a tiny cloud or a mass of fog move on its own. It was flying or gliding quickly across the road and just disappeared on the other side of the road. It moved straight and did not weave or bobble. We only saw it for maybe 5 seconds. I had never seen anything like it before and haven't seen another one since. I never reported it but I always remembered my sighting and was immediately struck by the similarity of what was reported in the UK." -PQ

Wisconsin Dogman?

"My girlfriend and I went out to feed deer for the hunting opener on Nov. 22, 2008. We were in the Chequamegon National Forest in northern Wisconsin. It was November 21, 2008 and the time was 12:10 AM, it was totally dark out and light snow was falling with an accumulation of about 1 inch covering the roads. The Temperature was 11F and the wind was blowing from the northwest with a wind chill of 0F. We made a U-turn to the left onto an unfinished ATV trail in one of our 4X4 Pickups heading towards last year's feed pile.

I got to the bottom of the hill and backed in and parked. I got out my pistol and loaded it, I then put it in my holster, I grabbed my headlight with three LED bulbs and secured it on my head, I handed her a shaker LED flashlight and proceeded to the back of my truck where I had a 5 gallon bucket with just under 2 gallons of corn and three apples in it strapped down with two of my ATV straps. I put the tailgate down, unstrapped the bucket and put the tailgate up. I walked around my side and then in front of the truck to her passenger side as she was putting mittens on. We both started to walk together, her just behind and to my right side when we both noticed a fresh set of tracks in the snow heading down wind of us in the same direction we were walking.

At first it was not the size that caught my attention; it was, *"What in God's creation made these tracks?!"* Immediately my skin crawled as I looked around with my head to see if what we just had come up on was in sight. I glanced back down in disbelief at the tracks. I was in a slight stage of shock as I looked at her she looked at me and we both looked down at four well-formed footprints of some kind of scary tracks that either of us had ever seen before. I sized my shoe beside one of the tracks and realized it was about 3 inches longer than my shoe which measures 12 inches heel to toe, and about 1 inch wider than my shoe which measures 4 inches at its widest width. Whatever we witnessed the foot prints of has two pointed talons on the end of its foot that are isometrically the same with a rectangle shaped heel. The talons joined on the outside and at the same length in between the talons on each foot. They are 15 inches long and 5 inches wide with 64-inch strides. I have a 36-inch stride at 5'10" tall to give an idea of the possible size of this creature, running or not we do not know.

I believe we just missed seeing what caused these tracks and what ever made the tracks was still in the area and possibly watching us. My girl told me to load my pistol and keep it out, I did not argue. At first she wanted to leave right away but the sheer adrenaline and interest of what caused the tracks I believe is what kept us there. I said "okay let's get out

81

of here" but again, interest kept us there looking at the tracks. My fear slightly subsided enough to think about the upcoming deer opener and decided I have the pistol and we will be okay. I started to walk the same way the tracks went up a hill on the trail when I stopped and looked back at her while she was still staring down at the prints. I said "come on let's get this over with" she caught up to me as we walked together, she said to me, "if this thing gets a hold of me put a bullet in my head" I thought about that as we kept walking. We went deep into the woods down a steep hill where I knew the feed pile was from last year. We got to where I wanted the pile to be, I took the lid off the bucket and dumped the corn and apples out and stepped on the apples, I snapped the lid back on the bucket and said "let's go"

We started to climb the hill when I realized we were off track and had to walk left to reach the trail to get back to the truck. I started to think that this was the scariest thing I have ever encountered and felt panic over coming me. I knew where I was and finally we got back on the trail and walked down to where we could see the tracks of the creature again. We both stared at them for about five minutes. When we got back to the truck just 20 yards from the prints, she got in and closed her door. I went behind the truck, opened the tailgate and re strapped the bucket down and closed the tailgate. I got to my side of the truck and took the clip out of my gun and got in. I threw my head light off my head as we drove away thinking and then I said, "I am not coming back here" and she agreed. We were both scared and could not believe what just happened.

It was a month earlier and 1.1 miles walking through the woods from where we witnessed the tracks that a different friend and I were camping. I went to bed early and fell into a deep sleep. I woke up to the sound of my friend walking behind the tent and my first reply was "what are you doing back there?" I woke up a little more and realized my friend was sleeping, breathing kind of loud next to me. I sat up against my gear and grabbed my pistol and flashlight and sat there cold and scared in the dark. I woke my friend up and told him what I could hear and he said, "Ah it was probably a deer or something." The temperature was around 26F. I looked out the flaps of the tent and could see the fire had died down and it was dark out there. I stood up and told my friend that I was going to the truck to warm up and get some sleep. I asked him if he wanted me to leave the pistol and he said, "No, I'll be alright." I left the tent and walked to my truck about 80 yards away and started it up to get warm. I turned my lights on a few different times to see if what had walked by the tent was in sight. I did not see anything; I turned my truck off and fell asleep.

Whatever walked by the tent was bipedal and made two steps into my sound range and out again. I did not hear any other noise from whatever walked by. I looked around the next morning for footprints but leaves covered the ground and I did not detect anything. A little more than two years earlier, it was summer and I was at this same location riding my ATV alone, I stopped and got off walking down to a nearby lake and was looking at the water and how clear it is when I could hear up on the hill above the camp ground we had stayed at a huge tree snap and hit the ground with a big thump as branches snapped off it and other trees as it fell. I got back to my ATV quickly at the time thinking a bear or buck was up there and I was not sticking around to find out. Two months later that summer I returned to this spot again riding my ATV, I shut off the wheeler and stood around close by thinking about the last time I was there I was scared off by something. I was there about five minutes when all of a sudden I could hear branches snapping off of trees as whatever was breaking branches was coming down the hill closer to where I was.

I got on my wheeler never to return until my friend and I camped there a little over two years later in October. My first two experiences with this creature while I was alone made me think it was possibly a bear or a buck deer, trouble with this theory is that I have come up on bear a dozen or so times and every time, the bear is running as fast as it can in another direction and whatever was making the tree sounds was not running anywhere. A deer also runs away at the first presence of a human. Now that we witnessed these creatures' footprints I put the puzzle pieces together and realize that this creature is living in this area and it has probably been there for a long, long, long time. I have learned it means us no harm (yet). It only makes a sound when I am alone (tree breaking). It is always downwind of me (us). It is out in the day and or night. It can see in the dark. It uses the wind to its advantage every chance it gets. It can hear well. It can smell good. It waits until we are vulnerable to approach us when two of us are together. I could possibly have smelled it and did not know what I smelled. I (we) have put 4,000 miles in this forest on my Grizzly ATV through deep desolate, thick wooded, swamp, lake areas and have now proved to ourselves that this undocumented at this time creature is in fact out there.

I believe this to be what the Monster quest American Werewolf series TV show on the History Channel has shown to be the half Man-half Wolf "DOGMAN?" that others have actually witnessed. I know where this creature is living and plan on an expedition to prove its existence. I want to document this creature because I feel everyone that enters the forest has a right to know it is there and for other various reasons. I am open to any and all that would like to comment or ask questions in discussing my encounters with this creature(s)."

Cryptid Sighting, Garrett County, Maryland.

"Early morning, December 16, 2009 at approximately 1:30 AM, I witnessed a strange creature as I drove home from a holiday party. I live in western Maryland a few miles outside of Grantsville, MD. The sighting occurred only 1 mile from my house. I was completely sober since I cannot drink alcohol for medical reasons. As well, I was not tired since I had slept several hours before I went to the party. I was alone, though I had given a friend a ride to her home. I was traveling at the posted speed limit, maybe a bit less since I always watch for wildlife crossing the road after dark.

I slowed down because there appeared to be an animal digging in some trash next to the right sight of the road. It was 20 feet or so from my car. I slowed down to get a better look and noticed that the creature was too tall and bulky to be any animal that I have ever seen locally. I'd say about 4 ft. tall and about 80 lbs. It was dark gray in color with long straight, coarse hair. Then it turned and stared at me with its large eyes set forward on its face that appeared bright red in the headlight. The paws were very unusual, almost like human hands with long fingers. It acted surprised that I was there but remained motionless staring back at me. The face was shaped a lot like a large rat but had a flat face. I didn't notice a tail.

After several seconds it crouched down on all fours and scampered off in a long gait towards the woods nearby. I decided not to chase after it since I had a bad feeling about this thing. I told a police officer friend who told me that there was a similar sighting the winter before after a homeowner witnessed it feeding on a deer in their backyard. He said that I should file a report with state wildlife officials but I wanted to see if anyone could suggest an identity of the creature before I file the report. Thanks for your site. I hope you can post this. I'll watch for opinions."
-D, Garrett Co. MD

Bear-Like Creature in Illinois.

"A few years ago, my now ex-wife and I were coming home from a trip to Vincennes, IN. It was around 10:00pm and in the late spring. We were traveling north on ILRR 33 towards Palestine, we lived in Robinson, IL. Somewhere just south of the "Fuller Cemetery" I spotted a wild turkey or some other large bird on the right-hand side of the road. As we past it, she started to scream. She worked herself up to nearly tears and I was laughing (I'm so mean), but I could tell she was honestly distraught. As I pulled over into the cemetery drive, I told her to calm down, it was just a turkey that we saw. I asked her why she got so scared. She said, "I didn't see a turkey!" I asked her what she saw and her response gave me goose-bumps. The hair on the back of my neck is standing up now, years later, re-telling the story. "What do you mean!? What did I see? You didn't see that?" I had no idea what she was talking about, but she told me just as we came around a small curve (where I had seen the turkey that she didn't see), that she saw a large animal running alongside our car. "All I could see was dark fur and red eyes. Its head was at the top of the window. It was humongous!" I started going through animals that were big and near that height. The only half-way logical one I could think of was a bear.

So when we got home I photo-shopped a picture of a bear illuminated as she would have seen it and reddened the eyes just a bit. She was frantic again, "that's what I saw...that's what I saw!"

Crawford County is not known for its bear population, in fact, other than this story, I've never heard from anyone else who has encountered one. They just aren't here. She would probably swear today that it was what she saw." -J.

Unknown Flying Entity.

"The encounter occurred on July 6, 2005 at about 11:30 pm. I had a long day in San Diego then afterward going to the beach at Del Mar, CA for some surf fishing. I arrived at my home in San Marcos about 11:00 pm. After cleaning my fish and showering, I was very tired. I went out to my carport for a smoke and a look at the night sky. I looked north, thinking about a recent UFO sighting and wondering what it's all about. In the distance, at a couple hundred feet, I saw a faintly visible moving object that flitted from side to side. Whatever it was, it reflected light from the streetlights. Its side to side movement was so fast, I couldn't tell if it was one object or two. The object then zipped directly over my neighbor's house across the street.
By this time, I was certain I'd never seen anything like it. It continued to move side to side, in a space of approximately 50 feet. It then stopped and I observed it more clearly.

It had big "eyes" and wing-like appendages, and was probably 2 to 3 feet in width. It remained still and I could see wavering reflections from its "wings" which were not beating like a bird's, but showed shimmering reflections from the streetlights. I felt the hair on my head rise all the way down my back to my ankles! It appeared to be looking at me, as I smoked my cigarette. I felt threatened, and said out loud, "I see you!" Then it went from stationary to out of sight, right over my head in an instant. I came out from under my covered carport, and turned to follow its movement. Immediately, it zipped into view directly above my head, obviously studying me! I could see really weird large and intensely dark "eyes." It seemed surprised by my looking right at it. It didn't like being seen. My apprehension rose even higher. It turned away and disappeared like a shot.

It had a birdlike shape, but was thicker. My impression was of reflections of the streetlights on wing-like appendages, and big dark eyes!

It wasn't a bird, bat or any familiar nocturnal creature. Its movements did not seem explicable in comparison to any creature that fly's by beating its wings. The hills and mountains are so rugged and inaccessible near my home, that anything could remain hidden and make night time forays at will. I read about "thunderbirds" but I'm not sure if this was one of these."

Are There Hobbits Among Us?

"Hello, Sir. My name is Dee and I would like to confide in you an experience I had in 1990 when I lived near Cooperstown, NY. It was mid spring and a girlfriend and I decided to take a walk in the surrounding countryside. While we were taking a rest near a large outcropping of rocks, there was a 'humming' sound coming from one of the nooks. My girlfriend stood and started walking toward the noise. Though it was late afternoon and we were in heavy tree cover, there was enough light to see into the rocks. As she got closer, she said that the sound was coming from inside one of the large boulders. I began to walk toward her and the boulder to listen for myself.

We stood there for about five minutes when we noticed the boulder seemed to 'shimmer' like water. We quickly stepped back as the shimmer grew and change to a greenish hue. Then suddenly, two small beings emerged from the shimmering portal. The beings walked towards us as we tried to move away but were paralyzed and unable to talk. These beings were about three foot in height and had green colored clothes that looked like work overalls. The faces and body features were human-like though I'd have to say more like human children but with some adult features. They also had long blonde hair and very dark, large round eyes. Their hands had four distinct fingers and were very rough textured. (This incident occurred much earlier than the film, but these beings remind me of the Hobbits in 'The Lord of the Rings,' sounds nuts, right?)

They took each of us by the hand and started pulling us toward the rock. We both quickly regained our ability to move and broke away from their grasp. As we ran down the hill, we could hear them running behind us. A minute or so into the chase, I felt something hit me on the back and realized one of the beings had thrown a stone at me. I stopped and looked back, but they were gone though I could hear voices from a distance that sounded like there were more of these beings and the sounds were getting louder.

We continued to run until we reached the car, got in and sped off. We had driven about a half mile when a piece of tree branch soared out of the woods and hit the side of the car. I looked up into the woods but neither of us could see any sign of the beings.

We were both shaking when we arrived home. We agreed not to tell anyone about the incident though I think she may have mentioned it to a friend (after we went separate ways) because there was talk about little people in the surrounding woods. I never had another encounter with these beings but I feel that they knew where I lived. One morning, I found a small pile of stones on my patio picnic table with a small four-fingered muddy hand print beside it.

I recently moved out of the area, but I still have a feeling they know where I am. Last week, I was leaving for work and walking to my car. When I got into the car, I noticed a reddish colored four-fingered hand print on the windshield. I took a closer look and realized that the hand print was made in blood. That evening, while sitting in my office at home, I heard voices outside. I looked out the office window and caught a quick glance of something darting into the bushes next door. I continued to watch, but didn't notice anything further.

I have no idea what is happening though I do know that I am not imagining any of this. Is there a possibility of little beings (ex. Hobbits, elves) living among us? I've never seen or read about any of this. It just seems so crazy. Any ideas?"

Winged Manta Ray Shaped Cryptid, Near Ashton, WV.

The following report was the first I received in regards to this phenomenon. Over the years, I have received subsequent sighting reports:

Date: Dec. 3, 2004.
Time: 6:00 - 7:00pm.
Weather Conditions: clear and already dark. Moon had not risen yet
Location: Traveling south on Rt.2 in WV from Point Pleasant to Huntington, WV. Near Ashton, WV.

"A friend and I were traveling on Rt. 2 towards Huntington, WV. I was on my way to set up my booth for an art show and my mind was occupied with the booth set up and show logistics. We had just gone over the railroad tracks outside of Ashton WV and were on a long straight stretch of road. There was distant oncoming traffic and the headlights were on. There were no cars behind us in sight. I was in the passenger seat and my friend was driving. I noticed a sudden movement in the sky over the Ohio River to my right in front of the car. It was a grayish, smooth, winged shape. The shape swooped in a figure 8 in front of the windshield and then was suddenly gone to the left of us. It didn't fly out of sight, it was just gone. This happened very quickly, but as I am a visual artist, it was impressed into my memory banks!

Size: Bigger than the car. The wingspread was wider than the 2 lane road we were on. The wings seemed to stretch wider somehow as it did the figure 8 swoop. It was never more than 25 feet away from us as it flew towards the windshield. We thought it was going to crash into the windshield! At one point during the swoop it was only about 5 feet off of the pavement.

Color: Grey, translucent like a jellyfish. As it banked and swooped I could see many angles of it and somehow it looked more transparent as it turned some parts to us. I immediately thought it was like a manta ray. The body was flattish like a manta ray or a bat. The wings were long and smooth and sort of pointed at the tip. I saw no texture or roughness on it, only smooth surface.

Characteristics: Only body and wings, no head, eyes, tail, or feet. It did not look humanoid in any way. On the other hand, it wasn't a bird either. It moved more like something in the ocean would move, Did not flap the wings like a bird, or flutter them like a bat, but stretched them instead. My friend (who alas passed away a year ago) said to him the wings looked ragged like there were pieces coming off of them.

He also said he got a good look at the underneath and it looked grey and smooth. This absolutely was not a machine! It was articulated like a living creature and seemed like something organic.

As I look back on this sighting, I wonder if it was something playing with us, It happened so quickly that the only scary part was when we thought it was going to crash into the windshield. It was so beautiful and strange! It reminded me of a sea creature more than anything else; maybe our air is like water to them.

The only other time in my life I have ever seen anything remotely similar was in 2000 in Clay Co. WV, driving along a one lane road along the Elk River (a river was present in both instance, I just realized) In that case, I was alone and for about a mile as I drove, I kept noticing a shimmer in front of the car about 15 feet ahead of the car. This was late morning in the summer. It preceded the car at the same distance for several minutes, then I noticed a shadow on the road too, large and shaped sort of like a bird. I looked up out of the windshield and there was a large crow flying above me. But what I first saw in front of the car was not a shadow, it was a disturbance in the air in front of my car that looked like a heat mirage sort of but was very close. This was a curvy country road right by the river. I had never seen heat mirages on that road before or since. At the time I thought that it was just sort of weird, then very close to that time I had a very lucid dream that I was in my car flying over the river right near the place where I saw the shadow.

As an artist, my mind is open to many possibilities and explanations, I think the unseen world is just a small vibration frequency away. As a child I was fascinated by fairies and nature spirits and spent a lot of time alone outdoors."

[Note: though there have been several variations in describing the 'Mothman,' this particular description is unique and most likely represents another cryptid or non-terrestrial entity. As well as the Mothman sightings, the area along the Ohio River (southern Ohio and southwest West Virginia) has had a large number of other paranormal events including UFOs, large apparitions and hauntings, native and folklore based creatures, etc.]

Flying Translucent Ray-Shaped Cryptid - Hampton Bays, New York.

My name is Jeni and I live in New York; I grew up on Long Island and have always loved heading out East, the Montauk Projects, Brookhaven Labs; we've had a lot of experience with the unexplained out here (I've seen a plethora of various types of UFOs on LI since early childhood). I stumbled across your blog and am writing in response to the post 'Winged Manta Ray Shaped Cryptid, Near Ashton, WV, 12/3/2004.'

Date of Event: July, 2006.
Time: 9:00 - 10:00 pm EST (estimated time frame).
Weather Conditions: Clear, bright night. The moon was very bright and large and you could see every star as the further east you go, the less 'light pollution you experience.
Location: Traveling West on Dune Road, stopped at the Jetty in Hampton Bays, NY (the end of Dune Road).

"My experience occurred sometime in July 2006, right after my father had passed away. I regularly take long drives out to the East end of Long Island and walk on the beaches at night as it's very peaceful and isolated. The beach in Hampton Bays (the Jetty at the end of Dune Road) is particularly nice at night. I've been there at least a hundred times and had never experienced anything out of the ordinary. I took my then fiancée out there to show him the phosphorescent shrimp that wash ashore as he had never seen them; we parked the car and proceeded to walk down to the water. The moon was very bright that night, so you could look down the long stretch of beach and see everything. We were alone. No other people were on the beach, no other cars were parked nearby and all establishments were closed; it's a rather remote area aside from a few scattered private residences and a few restaurant/bars. Now, a bit about me: I'm an artist, was raised with an open mind, am a healthy skeptic and I don't scare easily.

As soon as we stepped onto the beach I had a feeling of general unease; that instinctive fear that one would experience in the presence of a predator. I chose to ignore it; occasionally peeking over my shoulder at the long, empty stretch of beach behind me but mostly focusing on the tiny glowing shrimp beneath our feet. At one point I felt a presence and again, chose to ignore it as I've dealt with that quite a bit in my 30 years. I had not voiced my unease to my fiancee, so he was completely unaware. About 5 - 10 minutes into our short walk we were both hunched over, his back facing the jetty, mine facing the stretch of empty beach when he started peering over my shoulder, up into the sky. Perplexed, he'd look for a second, and then look away, at this point I was still trying to retain my composure and not look. Finally, after a few minutes, he looked over my head and yelled "oh my god! What *is* that?!" I turned to look and 'flying' directly over my head was this huge creature I'd never seen! I will detail as best I can:

It appeared translucent/transparent; no color whatsoever, no visible structure outside of the motion which indicated what it looked like; now, I myself am a visual artist, so this left a very distinct impression on me. This 'creature' was shaped and moving in the way a Manta Ray would; yet completely transparent! No color at all; I could see the stars through this thing; the only thing to allow the structure any appearance was the moonlight shining somehow on its' exterior!

It was larger than a standard sedan. Its wingspan was at least, from what I could estimate, 10' in width; while it was 'flying', its wings moving up and down. The movement seemed familiar, like that of a gull swooping down and hovering over the shoreline. It was approximately 10 - 15' over my head; it had no visible 'head' or 'tail'; no discernible limbs or appendages of any kind. It appeared and moved exactly as a Manta Ray without the 'Cephalic Lobes' or tail. I was completely awe-struck, but that fear took over and after about 30 seconds of staring at this thing we both turned and bolted toward the car. While running, we both simultaneously jerked our heads to the right in response to a glowing green light which seemed to flash twice (it was not the light from the tower on the jetty, nor was it from any boat; that water was clear). I never looked behind me. We started heading back on Dune Road when we saw what I could only describe as two, smaller 'rays' which moved more like a bat would, flying together from right to left overhead past the car. These two were translucent and had a grayish color to them. Strange. They were flying in the direction of the beach, where the larger, more transparent creature was. On the ride home, we spoke about how confused we were, but didn't compare notes on what we had seen, I told him I wanted to wait until we got home to do that.

Now I consider myself a well-educated believer in Supernatural / Paranormal phenomenon and have a long-standing fascination with Cryptids but I always approach everything with a healthy dose of skepticism. As soon as we arrived home, I tore two pages out of a sketchbook, grabbed two pencils and gave one of each to my fiancée, instructed him to draw exactly what he had seen and left the room; I did the same. When we were done, we placed our sketches side by side and they were identical. That was enough confirmation for me. I immediately went online to try to research any reports which would help explain what we had witnessed, but I couldn't find anything at all! It was extremely frustrating. I did report the sighting to the National UFO Reporting Center but still, until I stumbled across this post, was at a loss for any confirmation or additional reports of this type of creature.

I really would love to hear of anyone else who may have experienced something similar on the East end of Long Island. Feel free to post this if you like. I'd love some answers as I'm fascinated by this event. It's so difficult to describe the appearance due to the fact that it was transparent, yet we could see the motion. Almost like when heat rises from asphalt and wrinkles the air. I really was amazed and have no idea what this thing could be!

"It was so beautiful and strange! It reminded me of a sea creature more than anything else, maybe our air is like water to them." I feel the same way; I instantly felt that it seemed to be 'swimming' through the air. I also believe that it's possible that multiple dimensions are simply a vibration away; that many things are likely coming over and going back from time to time" -J

'Flying White Sting Ray' Sighting - Hebron, Kentucky.

"I am a sophomore who lives in Hebron, KY very close to the Ohio River. On January 25, 2012 around 9:00 pm I was in the car (my mom was driving) going home. It was dark and we were driving like normal. Then she stepped on the brake because a white stingray flying creature about 1 - 2 feet across swooped down and flew about 4 or 5 feet in front of the car about 5 feet off the ground. Two cars driving in the opposite direction also hit the brakes for it. Right after we saw it I thought it looked very strange but I thought I was just over exaggerating until my mom seemed to be startled by its weird stingray appearance. I then got the idea it might have been something different. It definitely was not a bird because it didn't really flap its wings. It looked like it was swimming underwater. Plus, it didn't seem to have a head from my perspective! I looked up what it could possibly be and found reports of the exact same thing (only bigger) a few years ago. The similarities are astonishing."

Strange Encounter in Cheboygan County, Michigan - Is the 'Dogman' Back?

"Hey, I'm Mike from the Cheboygan, MI area. This is true what I am about to describe. On November 24, 2010, two of my friends and I went out at night around 12 am. We were not hunting but had weapons. We were looking for a spot to set up our blinds for the muzzle loading season when we crossed from a field with tons of deer beddings. We came into another field with none whatsoever. We continued through this field and came across some kind of game trail. We decided to venture down this trail into the woods.

We got maybe 300 yards back in it and started hearing heavy breathing and snapping sounds in the thick brush to our right. We thought maybe coyotes but we got to a corner and were stopped in our track. In front of us, maybe 60 yards away, was something blacker than the woods standing on two feet and stood between 6'8" and 7'4". We slowly turned away and back tracked. Before we got to the field the same thing was in front of us again. We turned around for a second and then turned back, it was gone.

When we got into the field we noticed there were four or more of these creatures, one on each corner of the field just standing there. We saw one move halfway behind a tree. At this point we were freaking out. We made our way through the field and got to the edge and there was one standing directly in the middle of the trail entering the woods. We hauled butt back home and the whole way we felt like we were being watched and stalked.

We have been out every night since then. We have learned do not use lights because it comes closer than 60 yards. The closest it has been to me was maybe 25 yards and was moving closer. At that point I shot at it. There were a total of five that we saw the first night and after I shot at one. We went out last night and there were only four and they seemed more aggressive. In the field, it seems they tried herding us into a corner.

You can believe this or not, but I am in the Michigan National Guard and I put what I saw on my warrior ethos and army values."

93

'Dogman' Sightings - Baraga County, Michigan.

Back in July 2009, I received the following report in reference to at least two sightings of a supposed 'Dogman' in Baraga County in the Upper Peninsula of Michigan. I contacted the witness who seemed very truthful and credible:

"Last fall, my son and I were driving on US-41/M-28 towards Three Lakes in Michigan's Upper Peninsula (where I live). The beast ran across the highway near Tioga Creek. I had not heard of this before reading Phantoms and Monsters, but this is exactly what we saw. We are familiar with all animals living here. Moose regularly cross in front of drivers, so we watch the sides of the roads carefully. We were very puzzled and thought it might be some mutant wolf and could not figure out what we witnessed. It ran fairly fast about 50 feet in front of our truck. It was so strange because the front of it was much higher up than the back, larger than a wolf. It was very strange to see it on your website."

I contacted the witness and asked for any further detail of the sighting. This is what I received:

"It did not look exactly like the video or drawings I saw, but VERY close. The side view shape of the animal was almost like an ape shape, with the front legs longer than the back legs which made it run funny. It ran like a bear runs, with the exception of the back legs being shorter if you can picture that. The front, from the angle I saw, looked like it must have had a wide chest. The head appeared wolf-like, but it definitely was NOT a wolf. The color was brown and black mixed. The hair seemed med-long, like a wolf, and I remember thinking it might of had mange, must of had patches of hair missing.

I was telling my son, who is 13, about what I had found on your site and asked him what he remembered. He gave the same description, how very strange and out of place it was. He said that this spring he saw the same type of thing on a logging road near our house (I do remember him telling me that at that time) and it was the same thing. He was riding his dirt bike (we live in an extremely remote area) and it ran across the trail. I know where he is talking about because I pick berries there and do get a weird feeling like something is watching me. A neighbor told me that area is "Bigfoot Central", which I did not know or believe. But after doing further research today, there are a lot of reports of strange creatures in this area that go back many, many years.

Who knows what it is, but as long as it's not hurting anything, I hope it is left alone. I am very familiar with the wildlife. I do hunt and know

94

my tracks. I have not seen any strange tracks, but now will really keep my eyes open. Please keep me informed if you get any other reports from my area. -R."

The Stalker.

"Hi, I was wondering if you could offer your thoughts on my experience. My fiancée and I live in the mountains of Arizona and we went night fishing at an old fish hatchery, now privately owned ponds, tonight. We were there for a couple of minutes when we started to hear something rustling around at the pond next to us. At first I thought it was just an elk (we'd been there a couple of days before and there were tracks in the mud on the shore) but my fiancée was worried that it might be something else so he made a fire to try and scare it away. After a while the rustling stopped and we relaxed.

Not long later we heard a huge splash from the other pond. We thought that maybe a mountain lion or bear had jumped in trying to get some of the fish, as unrealistic as that seemed, but we never heard any more splashing and it was very unlikely that there was a fish the size of a full grown man in the pond next door. We didn't hear anything after that for a long time until suddenly there was another huge splash in our pond, but I couldn't see where it had come from or what had made it.

I was starting to get creeped out and the fire was dying out and I wanted to leave but my fiancée wanted to stay and fish some more. We could hear some more rustling in the reeds near us and suddenly my fiancée just started packing things up and dousing the fire and told me that he was ready to leave. We had left the car up by the highway by the gate and walked all the way down the dirt road, through the meadow, and past some other ponds to get to where we were fishing, so we still had a ways to walk before we would hop the fence and be back at the car. Every couple of seconds he would look behind us and then start walking faster. He told me that he thought there was a bear by the ponds and kept looking back and getting more panicked and walking faster. I was too chicken to look back at what he was obviously looking for.

By the time we were almost back to the car I was practically jogging to keep up with him and he was making comments like "once we get over the gate we'll be fine." When we finally did make it to the car he kept looking back over the meadow and acting antsy until we were driving back home. When I asked him if he'd seen the bear he replied "I don't know what that was, but it wasn't a bear." He proceeded to tell me about the animal he'd seen and that had looked right at him while he stood on

95

the edge of the pond. He described it as being as big as a bear, but looked like a half dog, half crocodile mutation of some kind. He said it looked scaly and that they had looked at each other right at the same moment and the creature had almost all black eyes. He also said that he felt like he was being studied by it, like it was very smart.

We were a little ways away from the ponds when he started looking back and walking faster. He said that first he saw the thing sitting on the top of the hill by the pond looking at us. This freaked him out so he started walking faster. When he looked again it had come down the hill and was still looking at us, making him walk even faster and tell me the bogus lie about the bear (he knew very well what a chicken I am and that I wouldn't look back). When he looked again, it was in the field, still far away, but still following us. The next time he said it was on the road behind us, walking like a cat does when stalking its prey. This was when he started making comments about getting over the gate and freaking out over the lantern because it was starting to dim (he's a scout and I guess the theory is that if you have light with you it will keep most everything away).

I've never seen him so freaked out before and I didn't know if I should think that he was just seeing things? But he swears up and down that he saw whatever it was. So we came home and looked up "giant alligator dog sightings" and came across the Doyarchu. The descriptions of it sound amazingly accurate to what he told me on the drive home and we kind of freaked ourselves out wondering if the second splash in our pond would have been its mate. I do believe that he saw something tonight; he's also sworn that he's never going back out there again.

After my parents laughed at us they suggested that we go back in the morning and look for tracks, but he flat out told me no! I know that this probably sounds like just a crazy story; Doyarchus are supposedly mythical creatures from Ireland, as I understand it. I just don't know how to explain what he swears he saw and felt like was going to eat us."

Was It The Ozark Howler?

"I don't have any idea what I witnessed Saturday evening (5/28) but it was the most frightening experience of my life. My wife and I were camping at an RV park near Jasper, Arkansas and planned to be there for several days. We arrived early Saturday and got situated soon after.

My wife wanted to look around the area since she had never been in the Ozarks. I was born and raised in the mountains and was familiar with the terrain and wildlife. After we tinkered around the campsite we decided to take a short hike through a nearby valley. There were a few caves and caverns along the way but nothing where I would have guessed any large predator would be living. After walking for an hour we started to head back towards the RV park.

Not long after we started walking back down the trail something caught my eye on the right in a sassafras thicket. My wife sensed it as well and stopped to look in the same direction. I could see this dark four-legged creature moving back and forth slowly through the brush. We immediately started to walk at a fast pace back towards the park. This creature was moving along as well, keeping its distance, but tracking us. This continued for what seemed like 10 minutes until we reached the clearing.

We got back to the campsite very shaken and nervous. All my years growing up in these mountains and I had never seen anything comparable to it. From what I could gather it was very large, almost the size of a black bear but moved close to the ground like a cat. It was also very dark in color. We didn't say anything to others camping nearby.

The rest of the evening was very quiet and peaceful until around 2:15 am, we heard what sounded like a high pitched howl coming from a distance. It was loud enough to wake both of us and I noticed several campers were looking outside, milling around and talking as well. Someone said it was just a coyote, but that was not a coyote or anything else I had ever heard before.

The next morning we woke around 9 am. When I stepped out of the RV a woman walked up to me and asked if I had heard the howling. I said that I did and had no idea what it was. The woman, who was camping nearby, said that she believed it to be the 'Ozark Howler' and that there had been a few sightings recently. I knew the stories about the 'Ozark Howler' but never believed any of it.

Well, my wife wanted to leave ASAP. Now I'm not sure what to think. We came home today and I looked up the 'Ozark Howler.' There isn't much to go on. I read your blog and thought you may want to get the word out. Is it possible this creature may live?

[Note: Information on this cryptid is scant, as well, the history is vague. There are a few anecdotal accounts but nothing to really 'hang your hat on.']

I later received the following email in response to the post:

"I have seen this creature very close to Jasper, Arkansas. I have lived in the Arkansas Ozarks for over 20 years. I never knew what it was until recently doing research. And I do believe I know where they are. I first had visual sight of one was off HWY 65 on HWY 256, heading towards Welcome Home. When I saw it I couldn't believe my eyes, I had never seen anything like it, what shocked me the most and what was most memorable was the horns coming out of its forehead, very much cat like, but it was its face with its horns that really shocked me. I drove as if in shock from a car crash not believing what I saw, until I started doing research on the subject. For over 10 years, in a remote region close to Mountain View, Arkansas, you can hear the howl every single night, usually after midnight. I never knew it was until I did the research, it is very elk like, almost like a horn, but definitely a howl. If anyone is brave enough I can show you where exactly to go to hear this, and where I made visual contact."

'Praying Mantis Man' Sighting, Musconetcong River, Hackettstown, NJ.

I received this report in reference to a strange sighting in northwest New Jersey. I contacted the witness for more information. The actual correspondence follows:

"I have recently been doing research regarding an encounter I had about five years ago.

Fly fishing on the Musconetcong River in New Jersey with my boss, I saw briefly what I could only describe as "a Praying Mantis Man."

Although the water was clear, there had been heavy rains the past couple of days. We should not have been out there; the river was "smooth" but the current was exceptionally strong. I was leaning backwards and digging my heels into the the gravel but the river was still kicking me along pretty good. Sketchy navigating.

Please know, I am "privy to the paranormal" and always have been. Shadow people, ghosts, whatever. But what I encountered that day was not spirit. It was a "biological", living creature. But it disappeared into thin air almost as soon as I saw it.

For whatever reason, my searches at the time turned up nothing. But then by chance I came across an 'Alien Race' type video on YouTube and there in the artwork I saw what I saw: "Ancient Mantis Leaders." So when

I began searching "Mantis Alien" instead of "Praying Mantis Man," I found a lot more.

They say they are "Inter-dimensional," whatever that means, but I did not get that impression. No, this creature was cloaked and because of both my inate sensory perception skills and the particular physical circumstances at the time, (important), -I can add details if you are interested- I just "Caught it." Movement out of the corner of my eye to my left and there it was."

The witness offered this follow-up:

"Humanoid. Tall. 6 foot at least -no reference points- but I sense 6'6" - 7'. Moving away from me back up the bank. (I am chest-high in the river) The first thing I see was the 'grasshopper' thigh, but bending forward like a human. Then the whole form. He is looking at me over his shoulder, moving up the bank, astonished, amazed. What, that I am in the water in a strong current, that I can see him? But yes we lock eyes and this creature is astonished, I get the sense that he can't believe I am in the water, that he can't believe I have seen him, that I am not perturbed at all, something of all three, I still don't know- just astonishment and he is actually trying to get away from me and the water!

Triangular head. Huge, slanted black eyes. Just like a Praying Mantis. Its whole body was gangly, nobby (very nobby!), but you could still sense it was powerful, and no, I would not say it was a "Big Bug," it was definitely humanoid despite the mantis/insect qualities.

No, I did not tell my boss about this, who was in the water too about fifty yards behind me at the time. Being "privy to the paranormal" you just see these things and sort of go "okay." No fear, no nothing, but I do get the sense that my "whatever" attitude contributed to this creature's astonishment. Frankly, I didn't give the encounter much though until recently.

I can forward more details. I just believe now that this encounter was somehow very important."

I wrote back to the witness (I am not going to reveal a name at this time) requesting further detail:

"This took place in Hackettstown, NJ. The stretch of the Musconetcong River here is unusual in that its west bank borders Rt. 46, (a local highway, congested with lots of stores) but the east bank where we were fishing borders fields and farmlands.

No bank to speak of on the developed side, but the sloping bank on the rural side was high (ten feet?) A strip of trees about 10 - 20 yards thick separated the river from the fields beyond, but there was the occasional gap/path, each about 20 yards wide that allowed clear access to the river.

Like I mentioned, the weather had been bad the previous several days, and the sky was white and heavy. It was mid-afternoon.

When I saw 'The Mantis Man,' it was in one of these gaps, moving back up the bank towards the fields, looking back at me over its left shoulder. About 15 - 20 yards away.

So understand that it was several feet above me (I looked up at it) and framed clearly against that blank/white sky. Like a full ghost apparition, it was indeed clear but nevertheless nearly transparent and fading fast. Then it "evaporated" mid-stride.

Again, I stress the strong impression that 'The Mantis Man' was cloaked and I "caught it" just right; it abruptly found itself against a "new"/blank background and was adjusting quickly. No, I do not believe it "slipped" into another dimension/plane.

I detected movement and first saw that strong left thigh, (and strong right calf) then the whole thing and immediately those eyes/face. The whole encounter was only a couple of seconds. I cannot tell you with any strong certainty what its feet or hands looked like, I wasn't looking there, but I can tell you that its arms were "normal," and not the literal Mantis forelegs I have recently seen in drawings of these "Aliens." That's really about it. Thanks."

[Note: was this possibly an alien being? This is definitely one of the strangest reports I have ever received.]

Large Bird-Like Creature Reported near Factoryville, PA.

I received this report of an incident that occurred on Monday, October 31, 2010:

"I was driving on RT 11 in Factoryville, Pa today around 2:45 pm. It was sunny out almost 50 degrees (41.56951, -75.79923) heading west.

I looked to the southwest in the sky, about 1/2 to 3/4 of a mile away, I noticed something in the sky and at first, I thought it was a hang-glider. It was shaped strange like a "V" flying backwards, and it had like a head and a neck sticking out.

Then I saw it turning really tight and was thinking how cool it looked. Then it started flapping its wings and it freaked me out. I never saw a bird that big especially from that distance before.

I was trying to slow down but there were cars behind me and I would have to go down the road and turn around and really nowhere to pull over to see it again. The shape while it was gliding was very strange; it seemed the wings tapered all the way down to nothing, not to a tail.

I'm 46 yrs old, lived and hunted in Pennsylvania my whole life and have seen turkey vultures, turkeys, great horned owls, cranes, and eagles. This seemed much bigger than all. If you can find out if there were any other reports similar, can you please email me, Thanks, -D."

Was It The Frogman...or Something Else Lurking in Loveland, Ohio?

I received the following anecdote from a woman who had a strange experience while living in Loveland, Ohio:

"We bought a little house down by the Loveland Castle Museum back in 2000. It was perched above a ravine and creek, and the back of the house dropped off very steeply. There would have been enough room for a man or a bipedal person to stand behind the house, but the basement windows were eye-level and the first floor was quite far up from the place where one could stand. The reason I point this out is that because it was a very small house, we had to use the basement for our two boys' bedroom. They kept complaining that "something" kept looking in the window at them and my husband and I laughed it off at first. It was a wooded setting, very rural and beautiful, and VERY DARK at night, having no streetlights out there. So it seemed funny that they were thinking something was watching them. We just told them maybe it was a deer (they are plentiful in the fall) and went about our business.

One night, however, I woke hearing a weird sound just outside our bedroom window on the first floor. It faced out back of the house, and I was puzzled as to what it could be because it sounded like a man, breathing heavily. I started to sit up and realized that whatever it was, it was looking in my window, just inches from my head and I was terrified. I did not look out because I knew that I would see it and I kept feeling something urging me to look. We often would hear squeaking noises, screeching (not like an owl) and a crying baby. I woke my husband up and he said whatever it was, it would have had to be 10 feet tall to look in our window. I couldn't sleep that night, but whatever had been there had moved on. I didn't mention it to the kids the next day. The boys came up from the basement, shaken from seeing "the red, glowing eyes" the night before. They were every bit as big as red road reflectors and they heard heavy breathing and the hair on their bodies stood up on end.

This was only ONE experience we had out there in Loveland. It's right down by the Little Miami River, only a stone's throw. Many weird things out there: green glows, orbs, something very large and black on top of the roof of the house very late at night (when light was shone on it, it did not go thru whatever it was on the roof, and it looked like a huge, dark figure.) I'd like to know if you have any more weird stories about this area. We moved a few miles away but still go past that area often. -C.F."

[Note: I assume that C.F. was not aware of the 'Loveland Frogman' sightings. I probably need to describe the incidents.]

The 1st sighting was in May, 1955, around 3:30 a.m. an unnamed business man claimed that he witnessed three bipedal, quasi-reptilian entities congregating by the side of the road. Later on March 3rd 1972, around 1:00 a.m. an anonymous police officer was traveling along Riverside Road heading towards Loveland, when he came across a frog like creature on the side of the road. A few weeks later on March 17, 1972, Officer Mark Mathews, reported pulling over to assist an injured animal on the side of the road. Upon approaching the creature Officer Mathews was startled by a strange Frogman like creature.

The story of the Loveland Frogmen begins on a barren stretch of road that runs along the Miami River in Clermont County, just on the outskirts of the small town of Loveland, Ohio. (This would probably be in the approximate area where C.F. lived). Around 3:30 a.m. in May of 1955, an unnamed business man claimed to witness three bipedal quasi-reptilian creatures gathered at the side of the road. The business man

102

pulled over to the curb and observed the creatures for what he estimated to be about three minutes. He went on to describe the creatures as being between 3 and 4 feet tall, covered with a leathery skin and having webbed hands and feet.

Perhaps the most distinguishing characteristic of these creatures however is there distinctly frog like heads, which the business man reported to have deep wrinkles where their hair should have been. As the anonymous business man watched the three "frogmen" one of the creatures suddenly held up with the witness described as some kind of wand above its head, he further claimed that sparks spewed out of the top of the wand. Upon witnessing this strange site the business man fled the scene fearing for his life.

The next documented encounter with the 'Loveland Frogmen' occurred at approximately 1:00 a.m. on March 3, 1972, when a police officer, who chose to remain anonymous, was traveling down Riverside Road heading towards Loveland. The officer claimed that he was driving slowly, due to overly ice roads, when he saw what appeared to be a dog on the side of the road. Suddenly the creature darted out in front of the cruiser causing the officer to slam on the breaks to avoid hitting the unknown animal. When the cruiser came to a stop the head lights fell upon a crouched frog like creature.

Quickly the creature stood on two legs stared back at the officer; its eyes illuminated by the high beams, and scrambled over the guard rail, down the embankment and finally vanished into the Ohio River. The officer described the creature as being 3 or 4 feet tall and weighing in the area of 50 to 75 pounds. He also stated that the skin had a leathery textured, and that the animal's resembled that of a frog or lizard. Later that evening another officer returned to the scene but found no signs of the animal, but did report that there where distinctive scratch marks on the guard raid that the creature reportedly scrambled over.

Another sighting by a police officer, Mark Mathews had an encounter of his own two weeks later. According to Officer Mathew's report he spotted what he believed to be an injured animal on the pavement while driving into Loveland. Mathews stepped out of his cruiser with the intention of removing the injured animal from the ice slicked road. As Officer Mathews got closer to the body the creature lurched upwards into a crouched position. Startled by the strange creatures frog like appearance, Mathews drew his gun and fired at the creature, wounded the "frog man" limped to the side of the road and slide over the guard rail. Officer Mathew's description of the frog like creature matched that of the other officers sighting two weeks prior.

Years after his original sighting, Officer Mathews has somewhat changed his story. He now claims that creature he saw that night was nothing more than a large reptile which had escaped from its owner. He further insisted that the reason he shot at the creature was to help confirm a fellow officer's story. Whether or not Mathews changed his story due to ridicule or a fading memory of an event which took place one dark night on an icy road outside of Loveland. In the many years following this small string of sightings there has been no reported sightings of the strange creatures which have become known as the 'Loveland Frogmen.'

Winged Enigma.

This is a case that I originally investigated in the mid 1980's:

Not long ago, I was thumbing through old investigation files when I came across notations I had made in regards to an unknown bird-like creature. The sightings were reported in 1985 and continued into 1987. It was an odd situation because I knew a few of the witnesses and I was also employed nearby at the time of the sightings. Cryptid investigation was new for me since my main focus was researching spiritual hauntings, but I had studied local Bigfoot encounters and wanted to expand my paranormal focus.

During the afternoon of May 5, 1985 I received a telephone call from Alfred M., the initial witness. He and 2 other men had seen a large bird-like creature perched in a hickory tree while driving south on Thistle Rd. toward River Rd. adjacent to the Patapsco State Park in SW Baltimore Co. Maryland. Alfred stopped the vehicle and watched the creature for several minutes. It eventually flew out of the tree and landed approximately 50 ft. from the road where the witnesses were able to get a keen observation of the creature. Albert stated that it stood 4-5 ft. high and was greenish-blue in color except for the head which was bright red. The wing span was enormous, he estimated it at 15 ft. or more tip-to-tip. The legs were thick and long with distinguishable talons. The eyes were also noticeable, slanted and large with a bright yellow hue. It also made 'clucking and cackle' sounds. After a minute or so, it unfurled its wings and took flight towards the east. Alfred said it reminded him of a hybrid 'dragon and peacock,' which he thought was crazy but he stuck with the description.

At the time, I thought that the creature was either a large turkey buzzard or maybe a peacock someone may have had as a pet. In fact, a peacock farm did exist in the area back in the 1950's according to people

I interviewed. I went to the location but found no evidence supporting the sighting.

Later that year, I had heard a rumor of a large bird being seen near the Hilton Area of the Patapsco State Park on Hilltop Rd. After several inquiries I was able to locate the witness, Darlene M., who confirmed the sighting. She and her daughter lived nearby and had been walking along Hilltop Rd. when they observed a huge bird flying towards them. Darlene stated that the creature got within 20 ft. of them then suddenly changed direction and flew into the woods. She said that they were terrified, she was sure it was going to hit them. She had gone to the library to see if she could find a picture of the creature. She found an old illustration of a Fung Hwang, or Chinese Phoenix and said it looked very similar to what they observed. She described the head was a vibrate red with fierce eyes. The wings were leathery and tipped with large green feathers. It flew by so quickly she was unable to get a better description.

Once again I was stumped by the sighting. I talked to two ornithologists who basically thought I was delusional. I also contacted the state park service and asked if they had heard of any strange reports. Nothing, though they were amused by the questions.

On the morning of April 29, 1986 several employees at the local paper mill observed a large bird standing in the loading area. According to the witnesses, this creature fit the description of a very large peacock...but there were some oddities. The head was red in color and it didn't have the long plumes. Other than those anomalies the overall description pointed towards a peacock. Could there be a breeding population in the state park?

In January 1987 a truck driver (Robert S.) was heading south on Thistle Rd. and was startled by a huge bird that flew across the road in front of his vehicle. I was able to interview him by telephone a few days later (he lived in Edison, NJ). His impression was that it 'looked like a dragon'. There was snow on the ground and the creature silhouetted well enough to get a quick but detailed look. Robert stated that it was 'as long as his truck was wide' and 'was powerfully built.' He also confirmed it had a red colored head and greenish-blue body and wings.

At this point I had nothing more than anecdotal evidence. There was no natural explanation for the existence of this creature. Even today I have little to go on because I simply have not come across another cryptid that matches the description.

The final sighting, as far as I know, took place on June 30, 1987. The

105

witness, David, was a Baltimore Gas and Electric employee who, along with his partner, was working along the power line that runs north to south through the state park. At a point north of Hilltop Rd. near the old mill village is an abandoned church graveyard. The former church was razed in the 1930's but the graveyard was left on its own...thus, it was severely overgrown by the woods. (I do think that the graves have been relocated since). David observed a large bird-like creature that he described as a 'gryphon,' though he admits that he didn't get a very good look at it. He only noticed the creature after hearing a rustling sound which he thought was probably deer moving through the woods. He said the creature rose up from a rock, spread its wings and vanished. David admitted that the sight of this beast was a shock and that he did not want to go back to the location.

I really wish I had more to offer. I kept the notes and vowed to go back and investigate the encounters if more sightings were reported. The witness Darlene may have been on to something, maybe this was a mythical firebird with the ability to be reborn from its own ashes. Unfortunately I have not heard of other incidents. Lon

Bipedal Canine Cryptid Reported Near Taylors Falls, Minnesota.

This report was forwarded by a witness in Minnesota who describes a bipedal canine cryptid. I have not discussed this incident with the witness so I'm presenting the sighting 'as is':

"Hello, I was steered to you by a man I know up north from here. He said that you are interested in these things so I figured I'd send an email.

I live in Taylors Falls, Minnesota and I was driving north on Wild Mountain Rd. around 7 am. On Jan 2nd. I was heading for the ski area when I saw some kind of animal running in the field towards the river. I pulled off the road and grabbed my binoculars. It looked like a large wolf but it was different. By that time some guy in a truck pulled up and was wondering what I was looking at. I told him that I think there is a large wolf in the field. He got out of the truck and asked to use the binoculars. He said he didn't think it was a wolf and that it looked like it was chasing something.

We stood for a few minutes watching. It would run into the woods then pop back into the field for a bit. The light was getting better so I grabbed my parka and started to walk closer to get a better look. The other guy said he had to leave but did say again that he didn't think it was a wolf.

I was about a 1/2 mile from the ski area near one of the trail roads. I started to walk towards the river. I was about 100ft from where I saw the animal from the road when I heard an owl screech coming from the woods to my right. On the edge of the woods this huge dog came running out of the trees. The best way to describe it was that it looked like a big hyena but it ran on two back legs and bent over. It had wooly black hair all over its body and a long thick tail. It must have weighed 200lbs or more. I've been in the woods all my life and have never seen anything like this. It looked over at me but continued to run from right to left in front of me. It also made a steady loud panting sound as it ran.

I turned on a pivot and ran out of there hoping this animal wasn't going to chase me. When I got to the car an old man had pulled off and standing there watching me. He wondered what I was doing. I yelled at him to "get the hell out of there" and said that a monster dog was out there. I think he believed me because the look on his face showed fear like he knew something was really out there.

I didn't go to the ski area, instead I went back home all shook up and asking myself what I saw. I read the stories about the Michigan Dogman and something you had about one being seen in Wisconsin. What do you think this was? It was no wolf or any other animal native to the area.

The guy who sent me your email address told me that there was a sighting last year just west of Duluth. He said it was a hunter that came across it while tracking a deer he had shot. I don't know the details but if it looked like the animal I saw I'm sure he got the hell out of there. Thanks -J"

Thunderbird Encounters, Illinois / Wisconsin.

The following report references two separate flying cryptid encounters in two different locations, within a two month period this past summer and by the same witness! Has anyone else seen something similar recently?

"This summer (June 19, 2011) I had two encounters with giant black birds; when I say giant I mean I saw (at two separate times) birds that were all black in color with wing spans as big as a small plane 14 feet or bigger.

My first encounter was early one summer morning when I was

returning from the Quad Cities. I was traveling on my motorcycle on Route 30 just past I-88 when I noticed a big black object in the distance sitting in the middle of the road. I slowed my motorcycle down as I got closer to the object. At first I thought it was a black bear sitting in the road but as I drove closer to the object I soon learned it wasn't a bear at all. The black object was a giant BLACK BIRD which stood at least 4 to 5 feet tall. I was in awe and a little bit scared at the sight of the GIANT BIRD. I stopped my motorcycle immediately hoping that the beast would not attack me. I then looked behind me in hopes of seeing anyone else who might be witnessing this amazing sight, but of course just like in the movies there was no one else on the road. Realizing it was just me and the GIANT BIRD, my heart began to race with thoughts of being attacked; I slowly pulled in the clutch and put the motorcycle in gear just in case I had to make a quick getaway. The GIANT BIRD heard the noise of the gear shifting. It then looked directly at me for a brief moment, swung open its massive wings (which were at least 14 feet long), stood up right, then leaped off the ground and took off in flight. The bird looked like a small black plane and when it flew by the trees the branches were swaying back and forth. I sat on my motorcycle watching the bird fly out of sight.

I still do not know what kind of creature it was that I encountered. I have been looking on line at several different species of birds but have yet to find the bird that I saw. The only bird that comes even close to what I saw was a condor but the bird I saw did not have a head like a condor nor did it look like that of a turkey buzzard or vulture plus this creature was much larger than a condor. I almost wonder if this was just a freak of nature; or possibly a prehistoric bird. Could it be possible that there are still some types of prehistoric birds still in existence? Trust me I am not crazy. I have recently seen pictures of the legendary Thunder Birds and that is exactly what this bird looked like.

My second encounter with a giant black bird was in August of 2011. My friends and I were traveling on our motorcycles near Lake Geneva, Wisconsin on some back road when all of a sudden a giant black bird appeared out of nowhere. The bird was obliviously mad at the noise of all of our motorcycles or something because it took a dive at the couple who were traveling in front of my wife and I. The giant bird actually dove at them causing them to swerve on their motorcycle. The bird then circled around them and tried to poop on them; yes I said poop on them! I wouldn't have believed it if I hadn't seen it with my own eyes. Luckily the poop missed them. I am not exaggerating when I say the stuff that came out of the creature was much larger than that of a human. It was disgusting! On a positive note there were ten of us who witnessed this giant bird. Once again none of us knew exactly what kind of bird it was that we encountered. Just like I had described before the giant bird was all black with a massive wing span and its head was not like that of a condor.

I couldn't believe that I was so fortunate to witness this massive bird again and I was so happy that my friends were with me to see it as well. I had told my friends about the bird that I had seen in June but I don't think that any of them really believed me. Now they know that I am not crazy and are obviously convinced that the Giant Black Bird does exist.

What is really kind of scary is that I do not believe that I saw the same bird twice; I truly believe that I saw two different birds that are of the same species. How I came to this conclusion is simple the first bird was bigger than the second bird.

I only hope that anyone who reads this takes this as a real encounter and just not as another fish story. I have ten witnesses to confirm one of my sightings. I only wish I had a picture too but obviously I can't take pictures while I am driving a motorcycle.

Oh well, believe it or not that is my story and I am sticking to it. Please let me know if anyone else has encountered one of these Giant Black Birds. Thank you, LF"

More Cryptid Bird Reports.

I received several large bird reports after the previous narrative was posted:

"After reading your article I wanted to share our encounter with you:"

Back in the Summer of 2002 during the late morning to early afternoon we were driving south on Highway 83 leaving Round Lake Beach, Illinois going towards Grayslake when we were startled something large and black crossing in front of the car and landing in small open area of brush to our left. One wing easily filled the entire view ahead of us.

We saw that one huge black bird had landed next to another one and that they were devouring what looked like a small deer or a large dog. It was just for an instant but they were prehistoric looking and larger than the local turkey buzzards. We watched the evening news thinking that some large vultures may have escaped the zoo but we saw no mention of any such creatures. We often wondered if anyone else had seen anything like these large black birds in northern Illinois.

Thank you for posting the article and letting me know that I wasn't the only one who saw this. *-S.R.*"

Big Black Bird, East Troy, WI.

"I used to live ten miles North of Lake Geneva in the East Troy WI area, and I investigated several reports of UFOs sailing over the rolling farmland and hovering low enough overhead to "hit with a rock," but never ran into any Big Black Bird (BBB) reports there.

However, my brother has had several strange encounters with weird things near his home in Providence, R.I., and one event that affected him the most was a sighting of two giant birds during a dawn fishing trip in Providence's famed Roger Williams Park.

As he was approaching one of the Park's larger interconnected lakes, walking across a tree-studded lawn surrounding a marble music temple, a pair of huge black "crows," with bodies as large as VW bugs, came swooping out of the early morning lake mist, flapping their enormous wings slowly as they swept between the treetops, curving past him thru the swirling fog, then twisting between the large shoreline oaks' intertwining branches and vanishing out over the lake!

They made no sound except the soft whoosh of air over their beating wings; their feathers were jet black, as were what he could see of their eyes; there was no odor. He froze in place as the apparitions flew past, then he rushed down thru the trees to the water's edge and scanned the lake's surface, but the creatures were nowhere to be seen, and never seen there again.

There are many other reports of paranormal activities in and around that Park over the years, including several experienced by my brother. Thanks *-W.*"

Huge Short-Snouted Snake-Like Creature, Ft. Myers, FL.

Sighting: January 20, 2012.
Location: SR 80, Ft. Myers, FL and I-75.
Time: 8:25 a.m.
Weather Conditions: Warm, bright sunshine, few clouds.
Duration of Sighting: About 30 seconds.

"I'm a department director for a county in South Florida. I was traveling with another director to a meeting. We were on Palm Beach Blvd (SR 80) near the ramp to I75. A traffic accident was blocking two of the three westbound lanes of SR 80, and traffic was backed-up and moving very slowly.

To my right was a small lake. While the general area is heavily populated, the lake connects to the Caloosahatchee River, and eventually to the Gulf of Mexico. On the other side of the river is a large wildlife refuge.

While sitting in traffic, my companion and I noticed a strange disturbance on the lake. I first though it was a fish jumping. However, the disturbance grew. She suggested it was a manatee or a dolphin, however, we ruled this out as manatees don't rise this high above the water, and there was no evidence of a dorsal fin. What we saw appeared to be something like a very large snake, I would estimate that it was close to the diameter of a telephone pole, though probably a little narrower, and could have been as much as 40 feet long. At sometimes it would disappear, and at other times it appeared as if it had multiple parts of its body rising out of the water at the same time. It looked almost like a very large snake, until it stuck its head out of the water. The head did not look like a snake's, it appeared to have a short snout. I did not see any fins, but my companion said she was certain she saw one fin. I thought the color of the body was dark grey, but the head appeared to be brown. It was approximately 400 feet away from us throughout the sighting, and it remained circling around one area. Eventually traffic cleared and we had to drive on.

I have lived in Florida for over 20 years. My companion has lived in South Florida all of her life. She and her husband have an offshore boat and often go fishing far out into the gulf. Neither of us has ever seen anything like this."

Huge Sloth-Like Cryptid Sighting in Southeast Georgia.

An associate forwarded an inquiry they received about a sighting in southeast Georgia:

"Last Autumn I caught sight of a large animal moving through the cypress trees of the swampy area that borders one of the fields I work. I live in Ware County, Georgia. I was working the field at the time and noticed the movement. It was late afternoon and still light out. The animal was huge, hairy and walked on all fours but I did see it rear up once. It reminded me of a black bear but much larger and lighter in color. I was about 200yds away from it but I still had a good look. I know for a fact that this was not a bear. I've seen black bears in the Okefenokee and this didn't look like one of those at all. I later saw a picture of an animal, (a Mapinguari) that is supposed to be a legend. I swear that is what I saw. Have you heard of this animal? I haven't seen it since but there have been a lot of cypress trees tore up lately and I'm wondering if it has been causing it. Some people have said for many years that there's a swamp beast in Ware County but I never paid it no mind until now. H."

[Note: The Mapinguari is a creature supposedly from the Amazon rain forests. Anybody familiar with a swamp-beast story in southeast Georgia?]

Has Bigfoot Already Been Found?

Is it possible that a Bigfoot or related hominid was found many years ago and remains hidden away from the public?

Near the end of the overnight appearance and discussion of Bigfoot by Jeff Meldrum and John Bindernagel on *Coast to Coast AM with George Noory*, September 21-22, 2006, an American, who claimed to be living in the Ukraine, telephoned into the talk-radio program. The credible-sounding individual had an intriguing account.

Without disclosing his name, the man identified himself as an environmental scientist. He stated that after the fall of the Soviet Union, he was hired to do air quality studies at the museum in the University in Leningrad (later St. Petersburg). While taking air samples in a three-level basement beneath the museum in 1992, he said he made a startling find.

The American scientist stated that he came across an object in a glass case that, according to the label, was an animal that looked like a Bigfoot, taken near a Russian outpost in northern California. The outpost was near Mendocino, and the mounted hominid was collected in the late 1700s, from what he could tell on the museum label. The huge animal had several layers of skin, exhibited a foot 17 inches long, and was a 7' 1" tall, hair-covered upright Bigfoot-like figure.

Could the Bigfoot have been collected by one of the first surveying Russian exploration parties?

Then there is the case of the Minnesota Iceman, a purported man-like creature frozen in a block of ice and displayed at fairs and carnivals in Minnesota and Wisconsin in late 1968. Two trained scientists, Ivan Sanderson (who was also a naturalist) and Bernard Heuvelmans (also a researcher and the founder of cryptozoology), examined the "Iceman" and concluded it was a genuine creature, noting "putrefaction where some of the flesh had been exposed from the melted ice." Heuvelmans wrote a scientific paper about the Iceman and even named it as a new species with Neanderthal affinities, *Homo pongoides*, and theorized it was killed in Vietnam during the war.

When the Smithsonian Institute was reportedly interested in the Iceman, Dr. John Napier was asked to investigate. He suggested the FBI investigate due to reports that the creature had been shot and killed. Shortly thereafter, the Iceman disappeared from public display, withdrawn, Hansen said, by the California-based owner.

Is There a Multidimensional Aspect to Cryptids?

Several years ago, I posted a poll on my blog that posed the question 'What is Bigfoot / Sasquatch?' To my surprise, 26% of the 574 participants answered they believed this creature was a multidimensional or extraterrestrial being. Are we at a point where people are open-minded enough to accept that a cryptid species may very well not be of our time or planet?

I posed this question to my readers and challenged them to make their case. Again, I was surprised at the amount of responses I received. A total of 112 emails, with well thought out theories and opinions, were received in a three day period.

I was sent a link to a piece written by paranormal researcher Nick Redfern that referenced a woman named Jenny, who had a remarkable tale about a creature she claimed to have encountered in a particularly dense area of Seattle woodland: nothing less than a fully-grown Saber-Tooth Tiger.

According to Jenny, she had been walking through the woods with her pet Labrador dog, Bobbie, when it suddenly stopped in its tracks, whined loudly, and dropped to the ground, shaking.

Thinking that it had possibly had a seizure, Jenny quickly bent down to comfort her pet, and could then see that the dog was staring intently to its left. Following the gaze of the dog, Jenny was horrified to see moving in the undergrowth what looked like a large predatory cat.

Assuming the creature was possibly a mountain lion filled Jenny with fear especially when its face could clearly be seen. The two huge teeth gave it the unmistakable appearance of a prehistoric Saber-Tooth Tiger. But then, high strangeness kicked in.

As the cat came into view and moved out of the bushes, she could see that its body had a semi-transparency to it. As well, the legs and paws were missing.

Jenny concluded that what she was seeing was not a still-living Saber-Tooth at all. Rather, she thought, it was a ghost of a Saber-Tooth that was haunting its former hunting grounds, many thousands of years after its death.

Could this be true? Are ghostly creatures from the past roaming our world? Perhaps the idea is not as far-fetched as it might seem. Our world cultures embrace thousands of legends that have been told for several millennia. It is conceivable that we are chasing ancient entities that slip in and out of our plane of existence.

I was told of the experiences of a veteran Sasquatch investigator in the California Sierra Nevada Mountains who stated that he was watching one of these creatures walk away from him and then suddenly disappear. The terrain did not offer cover or camouflage and there was no direction that the creature could have taken without being seen. There were no caves or holes for the Sasquatch to duck into, it just vanished.

Jonathan Downes, of the Centre for Fortean Zoology, first coined the term Zooform in 1990 and maintains that many of these phenomena result from complex psychosocial and sociological phenomena, and suggests that to classify all such phenomena as 'paranormal' in origin is counterproductive. Thought-form may be understood as a 'psychospiritual' complex of energy or consciousness manifested either consciously or unconsciously, by an individual or a group. Thought-forms are understood differently and take on different forms. My friend and colleague Rick Phillips states that anomalies and paranormal entities might fall into the category of 'Temporary Beings' and that these temporal characters represent ideas, including any type of cryptid. Could these entities be idea? Could they be ideas that transform into temporal characters - like memes? It's a concept that I believe is valid.

S.A. Robinson, a self-described 'armchair Bigfoot researcher' states that it's understandable that a subject as odd as this one, with the supposition that there is an enormous hairy creature that lives in forests around the country without being clearly photographed, videotaped or fully understood, should attract a good deal of divisiveness and even infighting. When proponents of the 'flesh and blood' camp mix with those who favor a 'magical' explanation, it can sour both sides from the real objective, which is to prove conclusively this entity's existence.

The principle of the simplest explanation, usually being the correct one, stands up in terms of building theories, but it should not be used as an arbiter between two opposing theories, and so we are left with the two camps.

He continues to explain that because of the similarities between our current understanding of the UFO phenomenon and that of Sasquatch, the fleeting visual aspect (most reports lasting less than a few seconds) the high strangeness (UFO's and Bigfoot moving at extreme speed often with disregard to physics) and with lack of much physical evidence (some trace material like radioactive soil or some unusual hair), not to mention the seeming invulnerability of both phenomena to physical attack (no UFOs or Bigfoot downed by gunfire) the link between Bigfoot and UFO encounters must fall into a similar category.

Why, in these modern times, with so much technology, do we not have a full accounting of everything in our animal kingdom? Some will cite the case of the Coelacanth fish as evidence of an evolutionary throwback that, due to its extreme habitat, was thought to be extinct until it was brought to fresh, modern speculation in a fisherman's net. To suggest that Bigfoot falls into this same explanation is to say that we have not really looked deeply enough into the woods. I refute this suggestion, as we have the ability to see nearly every square foot of the planet in high detail from space through satellite technology. We have a military/industrial complex that can ferret out any heat-producing organism of human size (or larger) with FLIR equipped cameras, and despite the large tracts of uninhabited land on the North American continent, humans have traipsed on so much of it that over the past fifty to one hundred years we have compiled perhaps several thousand decent eyewitness reports of weird footprints, strange sounds and sightings of the giant hairy extra-human entity.

A blog subscriber mentioned that just because we don't understand how Bigfoot move in and out of another dimension or what their purpose is, doesn't rule out this possibility. He has questioned a variety of people that channel multidimensional beings and every time the answer turns out that Bigfoot are indeed multidimensional beings as well. There are many other beings that can move in and out of another dimension including fairies, gnomes, sprites, and others. Indigenous people worldwide will verify this as they have strived to maintain to keep their connection to earth and the natural beings while the 'civilized' world has nearly completely lost touch. Only young children and intuitive adults are able to see/feel these beings as they move in and out of other dimensions. It's time for us to wake up to this possibility regardless of what conventional wisdom and science has to say about the matter. The evidence is there, time to become open to a broader perspective.

The late paranormal investigator Jon-Eric Beckjord's theories sum up much of the argument. He believed that Bigfoot and similar cryptids may be multidimensional beings that can occasionally take physical form for brief periods of time, but have the ability to 'fade out' and pass through 'wormholes,' possibly to other dimensions or parallel universes. He reported to have had one of the creatures speak to him using telepathy, communicating the words 'We're here, but we're not real, like what you think is real.' Beckjord claimed that such entities may be able to actually disappear into thin air, or even shape shift.

Beckjord maintained that the interdimensional hypothesis may possibly, if proven, explain why there are thousands of alleged Bigfoot creature sightings each year, yet no dead zoological physical body is ever found. This argument can also be made for many other cryptid beings. To evidence these ideas, Beckjord accumulated a large collection of enlarged photographs that he says show, among other things, 'half-Bigfoot' and 'invisible Bigfoot,' or possible aliens. The forms are often found in situations where the camera picked up images not seen by the witnesses, often due to distance. According to Beckjord, the images show primates, carnivores and beings not readily identified within known zoological classifications that resemble descriptions of aliens submitted to investigators. He conducted much field work, such as camping out at 'window sites' where, he said, Bigfoot activity is frequently seen. He collected his own photographic evidence of what he believes to be a 'tribe' of either Bigfoot or aliens at El Dorado National Forest.

Beckjord's strong beliefs about Bigfoot and similar entities brought him into conflict not only with skeptics, who consider Bigfoot sightings to be a cultural phenomenon purely resulting from wishful thinking or hoaxes, but also with those who believe Bigfoot to be a physical creature.

I received a telephone call from a woman in British Columbia who said she was the daughter of a Kootenai shaman. She stated that most Native tribes seem to believe Sasquatch is a non-physical creature. Some tribal elders mention that they have seen the creature shape shift into a wolf. She said her father thought that the creatures lived in another dimension from our physical plane, but can come here as it wishes. He also believed that Sasquatch has great psychic abilities and that the creature can be visible to some people, while at the same time remain invisible to others in the same group.

Maybe we'll discover beyond a doubt where the truth lies in reference to Sasquatch and other unknown beings. There may be a grand connection between all the mysteries in our world, possibly involving other worlds or dimensions as well. Mankind may be the greatest mystery of all and the reason why Sasquatch, extraterrestrials, spirits, etc. seem to be as fascinated with us as we are with them.

"While many cryptozoologists and cryptozoology supporters find such theories ridiculous, and often laugh them off, we would all do well to remember that the so-called "mainstream" of science has much the same reaction when presented with the possibility of Sasquatch existing at all. If we hope for mainstream scientists to keep an open mind, we must lead by example and not waste time and energy. That would be better spent searching for evidence, fighting amongst ourselves."
-James R. Harnock

Thanks for reading. Lon

32613589R00070